"*A Certain Sound* is a we
that was a joy to read. A
preaching, I thank God for this stirring call to the church to fulfil one of her
main duties—namely, preaching Jesus 'to every creature.' Read this book. Master it. And with the help of the Holy Spirit, let the 'certain sound' of the glorious
gospel of Christ be heard outdoors once again."
—Rob Ventura, Grace Community Baptist Church, North Providence,
Rhode Island, and coauthor of *A Portrait of Paul* and *Spiritual Warfare*

"*A Certain Sound* by Ryan Denton and Scott Smith is a welcome contribution to
the contemporary discussion on open air preaching. From a perspective deeply
grounded in the Christian tradition and Reformed and Puritan theology, Denton and Smith defend the ministry of street preaching in a firm but moderate
tone. Everyone who practices open air preaching or who is interested in its biblical basis must read this book."
—Sam Waldron, academic dean and professor of systematic theology
at Covenant Baptist Theological Seminary, and a pastor of
Grace Reformed Baptist Church in Owensboro, Kentucky

"Without question there is a resurgence of open air preaching in the United
States. I, for one, welcome it, but I know many others in the Reformed and
evangelical church world are highly skeptical. I too have observed many who
have given open air preaching a bad name and brought disrepute on the practice. For this reason, I have for some time wished someone would write an
apologetic for open air preaching, and I believe we now have such an important
book in *A Certain Sound: A Primer on Open Air Preaching*.

"The authors are seasoned open air preachers with whom I have preached
several times in the streets of America. They are passionate, Reformed, and
Christ-centered in their preaching. I urge pastors, evangelists, and laypeople to
read this book, and hopefully God will use it to lend credibility to the practice
and to inspire churches everywhere to get behind open air preaching."
—Al Baker, evangelist with Presbyterian Evangelistic Fellowship
and author of *Evangelistic Preaching in the 21st Century*

"I love this book not only because I know and have worked with one of its
authors personally, witnessing firsthand the lessons taught here being put into
practice and benefiting from that, but also because it is thoroughly biblical.
In my opinion, the authors make the case, theologically and historically, for
a return to the time-honored practice of open air evangelism. I hope seminary students, church members, and elders will read this book. By turns I was
encouraged, then convicted, but always blessed. May God give all of us the same
hunger to see the lost saved as the authors exhibit in this work!"
—Gabriel N. E. Fluhrer, associate minister of
First Presbyterian Church, Columbia, South Carolina

"The expression 'desperate times call for desperate measures' would be an adequate description for such a book as this. To the true church, this book will seem like fresh air and much-needed CPR. To the pampered, pretty-boy, American evangelical, this book will seem more like an affront and attack on their backslapping, worldly, man-pleasing, 'goodie-bag' attempts to reach the world with 'the gospel.' I would describe the book like this: doctrinally sound, refreshing, unashamed, unapologetic, and revivalistic! I would love to stick a copy of this fiery little book in every Christian college, church, and library in America."

—Jeff Rose, founder of JeremiahCry Ministries and pastor of One:16 Bible Church, Watauga, Texas

"Unfortunately, too many Christians have not been taught the important doctrines such as the Trinity, the gospel, regeneration, and justification. This has led to many unbiblical methods and catchphrases when it comes to open air preaching and evangelism. Ryan Denton and Scott Smith have provided a most valuable work in their book *A Certain Sound: A Primer on Open Air Preaching*. But this book is not merely for open air preachers. Every Christian will greatly benefit from the robust presentation, with its correct application of important biblical doctrines and apologetic necessity in evangelism—all written in a simple, comprehensible fashion. *A Certain Sound* is an indispensable work for laypeople, due to its sound and plentiful theological content, and for any open air preacher craving to glorify God in his public presentation."

—Edward Dalcour, faculty of theology, North-West University, and president, Department of Christian Defense

"Balanced, biblical, concise, articulate, and gracious. This excellent literary contribution brings wisdom and clarity to an often controversial work. Finally, a primer on open air preaching that both fills the vacuum of literature on the subject and provides sensibility to it. Ryan Denton and Scott Smith are to be commended for providing light to the important ministry of open air preaching that will help the preacher in his preaching and in his relationship with the church."

—Joe Jacowitz, pastor, Christ Bible Church, Pleasanton, California; and president of FirstLove Missions, FirstLove Publications, and FirstLove Radio

# A CERTAIN
# SOUND

# A CERTAIN SOUND

A Primer on Open Air Preaching

Ryan Denton and Scott Smith

**Reformation Heritage Books**
Grand Rapids, Michigan

*A Certain Sound*
© 2019 by Ryan Denton and Scott Smith

**Reformation Heritage Books**
2965 Leonard St. NE
Grand Rapids, MI 49525
616-977-0889
orders@heritagebooks.org
www.heritagebooks.org

*Printed in the United States of America*
19 20 21 22 23 24/10 9 8 7 6 5 4 3 2 1

Library of Congress Cataloging-in-Publication Data

Names: Denton, Ryan, author.
Title: A certain sound : a primer on open air preaching / Ryan Denton and Scott Smith.
Description: Grand Rapids, Michigan : Reformation Heritage Books, 2019. | Includes bibliographical references.
Identifiers: LCCN 2019002507 (print) | LCCN 2019004620 (ebook) | ISBN 9781601786869 (epub) | ISBN 9781601786852 (pbk. : alk. paper)
Subjects: LCSH: Open-air preaching.
Classification: LCC BV4235.O7 (ebook) | LCC BV4235.O7 D46 2019 (print) | DDC 251—dc23
LC record available at https://lccn.loc.gov/2019002507

*For additional Reformed literature, request a free book list from Reformation Heritage Books at the above regular or e-mail address.*

# Table of Contents

# Foreword

I am excited to see the publication of this book, for it is the first biblically balanced and theologically informed book I have ever read on open air preaching. Here you will find no zeal without knowledge, but rather zeal inflamed by love and directed by the Word of God. As such, it offers a corrective both to those sluggish to evangelize in public and to those who do evangelize but with rash and foolish pride that dishonors Christ.

Three factors make this book especially practical. First, it grounds evangelism upon Reformed theology, including the proper evangelistic use of the moral law and apologetics. This doctrinal foundation supports the open air preacher with God-centered wisdom and tremendous encouragement in trials. Second, this book addresses the relationship of the open air preacher to the local church. Too often, such evangelists act like rogue elephants—independent, vicious, and dangerous. Denton and Smith call for public evangelists rooted in the body of Christ and submissive to its leadership. Third, the authors offer good counsel for what the open air preacher can expect in different settings and how best to respond. This is crucial, for open air preaching will be opposed, and the preacher must respond to persecution in a manner fitting to the gospel he preaches.

May God use this book in churches, Christian schools, and seminaries to raise up preachers who will reach out more boldly and lovingly to perishing sinners outside the church's assemblies, and to stir up the whole church to support them in fervent prayer.

—Joel R. Beeke
Puritan Reformed Theological Seminary

# Acknowledgments

This book would be impossible and irrelevant without the Lord of Lords and King of Kings, the One "which worketh in you both to will and to do of his good pleasure" (Phil. 2:13). He alone deserves all the glory, so I dedicate this book to Him. I'm grateful for my wife, Tasha, whose simple devotion to the Lord humbles me on a daily basis. She is the best example I know of "a meek and quiet spirit, which is in the sight of God of great price" (1 Peter 3:4). I'm also grateful for my parents, pastors Joe Rosales and Jerry Minor, and all the men preaching the gospel in the open air, whose aim is to preach, die, be forgotten, and "endure all things for the elect's sakes" (2 Tim. 2:10).

—Ryan Denton

I dedicate this book to Christ Himself, the author and finisher of my faith. I love the Lord and long to bring Him some small measure of glory before He calls me home. I also dedicate this book to my wonderful wife, Patte. She is the greatest Christian I have ever met and has influenced so many believers to take up their cross, deny themselves, and get active in advancing the Lord's fame. I have been encouraged and strengthened by her companionship and example. She taught me, "You can't plow a field by turning it over in your mind." Finally, I am grateful to my close friend Bill Adams and other fellow street preachers: Ryan Denton, Mike Stockwell, Jimmy Hamilton, Robert Gray, Don Karns, Shawn Holes, and Bobby McCreery. They are the off-scouring of the world and the red-headed stepchildren in the body of Christ. The Lord Himself will own them on the last day.

—Scott Smith

# Introduction

This book is not an exhaustive analysis of open air preaching. The subject is too broad for such an endeavor, especially considering all the different ways to go about it. At the end of the day, we recognize there is no black-and-white approach. As with any kind of preaching, it must be biblical and bathed in prayer. But each preacher will approach the task differently. That is not to say there is no "right way" or proper theology when it comes to open air preaching. There is, and this book will demonstrate both.

As Charles Spurgeon and others have pointed out, no defense is necessary when it comes to publicly proclaiming the gospel.[1] Yet it is important to know that open air preaching is not some kind of whimsical or unbiblical method for getting the gospel to the lost, nor should it be treated as some idolized form of delivery. We by no means believe that everyone should preach in the open air, nor do we think it is necessarily the best or only method of evangelism. Likewise, we do not believe that open air preaching has more priority than pulpit preaching. The two should never be in conflict with one another. Open air preaching is simply a means of reaching people outside the church with God's Word.

We do hope, however, that this book answers critics or skeptics of open air preaching. The church and professing Christians often look

---

1. Spurgeon goes so far as to say, "No sort of defense is needed for preaching out-of-doors; but it would need very potent arguments to prove that a man had done his duty who has never preached beyond the walls of his meetinghouse. A defense is required rather for services within buildings than for worship outside of them." Charles Spurgeon, *Lectures to My Students* (Grand Rapids: Zondervan, 1980), 254.

down on it. Sometimes rightly so, but more often than not, the concern is unfounded. We hope that critics will approach this book with a patient openness to a method of evangelism that is seen in the Bible and throughout church history. We want them to see that it can be done in a proper, biblical way and that this form of preaching has harvested much fruit for the kingdom of God. We also desire that this book will stimulate more churchgoers and pastors to get behind their local evangelists. Oftentimes ignorance and bad experiences can taint our view of things. But a few bad apples should not spoil the whole bunch. Just because there are bad pastors and bad churches in the world does not mean all are that way, and it certainly does not mean that all pastors and churches should be dismissed. The same holds true for open air preaching.

We also hope this book can be useful to preachers across the world. A resurgence of open air preaching is happening worldwide: America, Canada, the United Kingdom, Mexico, and even India and South America are seeing preachers rise up on the streets of many cities. While only a few such ministers labored in the 1970s and 1980s, today a kind of revival is taking place when it comes to open air preaching. This is terrific, but only to the extent that it is being done in a proper way, which is why so much of this book focuses on Reformed theology, church history, the importance of the church, and the character and manner of the preacher. He cannot just "wing it." As encouraging as it is to see open air preaching done throughout the world, it is just as discouraging to see preaching laced with bad theology, disrespect for the church, and no regard for the manner of the preacher. This book seeks to be useful in these areas as well.

Lastly, it is our passion to see open air preaching being encouraged and taught at seminaries and churches across the country. We are aware of only a handful of seminaries in the world that encourage their men to open air preach. Budding ministers have no better preparation for some of the challenges of ministry than preaching on the streets. It will help them to mortify their flesh, fear, and pride—the constant enemies of every minister in the church. It will teach them how to respond to the rebukes of an unbelieving society, equipping them to defend the faith against cults, world religions, and the atheists of our day. Perhaps most importantly, it will help them to be better preachers in the pulpit.

Spurgeon encouraged his pupils to be active in open air preaching the moment they started pastoring: "One of the earliest things that a minister should do when he leaves college and settles in a country town or village is to begin open air speaking."[2] We encourage every seminary in the world to establish in their students a similar passion for open air preaching. We hope this book helps ministers and professors train pupils for such a task. Many are called to the work of open air preaching without any idea of how to begin. This book seeks to guard young men against mistakes we have made in our own ministries. It seeks to encourage the preacher to continue sowing the gospel in public despite the constant antagonism that will come against such a calling.

In the end, we recognize that no book could ever fully prepare someone for public evangelism. The best instructor is the Holy Spirit working through the Word of God. The best way to learn is to go out and preach. Some open air preachers may be more qualified than we are to delve into this topic. There are surely better writers. But by the grace of God we have experienced what it is to preach in the trenches on a daily basis. Ryan Denton is a Reformed Baptist and a graduate of Southern Baptist Theological Seminary. He has engaged in open air preaching as both a pastor and evangelist and is the director of Christ in the Wild Ministries, based out of El Paso and Albuquerque. Scott Smith is a graduate of Reformed Theological Seminary and an active Presbyterian. He has preached in the open air for more than ten years and has trained hundreds of preachers and labored with thousands more around the world. He is the director of Schoolmaster Ministries, based in Raleigh, North Carolina.

We have seen positive aspects of open air preaching that need to be encouraged and stressed, but we have also made and seen many mistakes that should be avoided. We have experienced the frustration of not knowing how to preach in the streets yet knowing we were called to do it. We know the disappointment when some pastors, seminaries, and ministries suggest that open air preaching should no longer be done. We hope this book is an antidote to such difficulties. At the end of the day, like evangelism, this book was like "a burning fire shut up in [our] bones" (Jer. 20:9) and had to be put on paper.

---

2. Spurgeon, *Lectures to My Students*, 275.

The title, *A Certain Sound*, comes from Paul's words in 1 Corinthians 14:8: "For if the trumpet give an uncertain sound, who shall prepare himself to the battle?" Paul is encouraging the church to speak with clear, intelligible speech whenever uttering God's Word. The same must be said for the preacher and, indeed, could be said for this book. We are attempting to make "a certain sound." As far as we know, there has never been a distinctly Reformed primer on open air preaching. This is an attempt to fill that void. We hope this book aids preachers to make a sound that glorifies God and magnifies His sovereign grace, that calls all people everywhere to repent and believe the gospel, that points preachers toward the high calling of making much of Christ, that advances the Lord's kingdom and brings honor to His name. Anything less would be a muddled message and a waste of time.

*SOLI DEO GLORIA*
GLORY TO GOD ALONE

# PART ONE

## THEOLOGY OF OPEN AIR PREACHING

# Chapter One

# A History of Open Air Preaching

*And they went forth, and preached every where, the Lord working with them, and confirming the word with signs following.*
—Mark 16:20

In a culture where pragmatic evangelism and seeker-friendly churches are in vogue, it is natural that many will think open air preaching is scandalous. Such people argue that this kind of preaching had a place in the past but that today, in our more "cosmopolitan" culture, we should use talks over coffee or casual Bible studies at home to share the gospel. These people claim it is necessary to build a relationship first in order to "earn the right" to share the gospel. People have changed, they argue, and so should our methods. Sadly, this is not a caricature. This view of evangelism is rampant in the Western church today. But it is critical to understand that society and even the church in general have never been accepting of open air preaching. It has always been shocking. Consider the following from a 2009 interview with Paul Washer:

> Spurgeon was constantly attacked in his culture for the openness of his faith and the openness of his preaching. If you go back to the time of Whitefield and just look at the political cartoons written against Whitefield, I mean, he was considered an absolute fanatic, a crazy man. Why? *Because he preached in the open air.* John and Charles Wesley in England, Howell Harris and Daniel Rowland. *It has never been with the culture to do open air evangelism....* It has been against culture since the moment the apostle Paul stood up

in that great coliseum and spoke the Word of God. It has always been against culture.[1]

Whether the open air preacher wears a suit and tie or a T-shirt and tennis shoes, whether his manner is boisterous or soft, direct or winsome, the natural man will always see such preaching as offensive. The church in general will see it as an affront. And from man's perspective, its fruit has usually been scarce. The apostle Paul was such a preacher. Far from being "successful," he was beaten, lashed, stoned, and rejected by Jews, Gentiles, and even professing Christians (2 Cor. 11:25). He was seen by most as vile and oafish. Paul and others have demonstrated that the offense of the cross and "the foolishness of preaching" (1 Cor. 1:21) is never so apparent as when one is heralding it in the middle of a crowd.

From time immemorial, civilizations of all types have used messengers to stand in public and announce news. God has designed man to hear messages and respond to them. People around the world preached and still preach out in the open to get their message to as many as possible. There is no need to dramatize or complicate or puff up open air preaching. It is merely a way for men and women to hear a word from God. Christ commands His disciples to go into all the world and "preach the gospel" (Mark 16:15), teaching others "to observe all things whatsoever I have commanded you" (Matt. 28:20). This is all that any kind of preaching seeks to do—get the message of Christ into the ears of the people.

Open air preaching comes down to us from a long tradition of men in the Bible who proclaimed God's Word in the public square. From Genesis to Revelation, God's servants are seen preaching without the aid of a pulpit or even a church building. This is not to downplay the importance of either of these. Every Christian should have a high regard for both. It is merely to show that the Bible never prohibits the ministry of open air preaching. On the contrary, it shows this to be the method most preferred by the saints of old. The reason for this is simple

---

1. Cameron Buettel, "Cameron Buettel Interviews Paul Washer," Sermon Audio, July 23, 2009, https://www.sermonaudio.com/sermoninfo.asp?m=t&s=723091214300 (emphasis added).

and by no means outdated. The preachers of Scripture found out where the lost were congregating, then went and preached to them. How superfluous man's ways are when compared to Scripture. Think of how many hours are spent strategizing about evangelism in classrooms and church meetings around the country. Think of the methods the Western church has come up with to win the lost to Christ. The Scriptures show us a simpler way: find the lost, then get the gospel to them. Open air preaching provides a way to get the gospel to a large group of people at one time and is designed to reach those who would not typically go to church or have a conversation about God.

Nowhere does Scripture give an explicit command to preach inside. In fact, with the exception of synagogues, only rarely do we find anyone preaching inside the confines of a building. This is the opposite of today's mind-set. Ministers and Christians often assume that preaching can only be done inside in a formal, prearranged way. Again, the pulpit ministry should never be denigrated. It is one of God's chief means for bringing the Word to His people. But in Scripture, open air preaching is the typical approach, not the exception, and it is rarely formal or prearranged. Spurgeon notes, "We are at full liberty to believe that Enoch, the seventh from Adam, when he prophesied, asked for no better pulpit than the hillside, and that Noah, as a preacher of righteousness, was willing to reason with his contemporaries in the shipyard wherein his marvelous ark was builded."[2] Some may argue that Enoch and Noah preached in the open air because they had no edifices to preach in or that if they had church buildings and pulpits in those days, the preachers of Scripture would have confined themselves to these rather than preach outside. Such speculation is irrelevant. Although we would never claim that indoor preaching is wrong, it would likewise be a mistake to assume that outdoor preaching is a secondary or lesser form.

Consider also the Mosaic era, in which preachers chose to proclaim the oracles of God in the fields, beneath the blue skies, even though worship was becoming more ritualized and the tabernacle was already erected. As Edwin Byington states, "Moses, during the time of his leadership, gave extensive and minute directions for public worship, but closed his ministry without having authorized the erection of a covered

---

2. Spurgeon, *Lectures to My Students*, 234.

auditorium for the worshipers."[3] If God had desired to establish a ritual for indoor preaching, it would have been while establishing these other rituals for worship. But God did not. Nor did things change with Joshua. Presumably all his addresses were made in the field. Likewise during the time of the judges and in the days of Samuel and Saul. We do not mean to imply that indoor preaching has not been sanctioned or approved by God. We merely point out that all of these men are shown to be delivering God's Word in the open.

David's and Solomon's reigns provide us with perhaps the best illustration of this preference for outdoor preaching. Dwellings were then permanent. The king had a palace. The temple was being planned and built. Yet religious addresses were still made outside. Even after the temple was finished, Solomon chose to make his dedicatory address out in the open. On this point Byington says, "The Lord had His Temple, with the holy place covered, the people had their houses, but the worshipers continued to assemble in the courts of the Lord's house and other open places, as their fathers did before them in the wilderness."[4] Solomon's wisdom books provide us with one of the most striking illustrations of open air proclamation in the entire Bible: "Wisdom crieth without; she uttereth her voice in the streets: She crieth in the chief place of concourse, in the openings of the gates: in the city she uttereth her words" (Prov. 1:20–21).

This argument is further confirmed when we turn to the Old Testament prophets: Elijah preached on Mount Carmel; Jonah preached in the streets of Nineveh with a simple, forceful message that brought the entire city to repentance (Jonah 3:1–5); Jeremiah heralded the words of God in the valley of Hinnom and in "the gate of the Lord's house," preaching sin and doom, proclaiming the very words of God (Jer. 7:1–3). Note that many of these prophets, especially Jeremiah, preached without the authority of the priests. Jeremiah was struck by one of the priests because of his message and even thrown into prison and a well. Although we believe that preachers should be sent out and held accountable by their local church, it is crucial to see that in an era when

---

3. Edwin Byington, *Open-Air Preaching: A Practical Manual for Pastors, Evangelists, and Other Christian Workers* (Hartford, Conn.: Hartford Theological Seminary, 1892), 9.
4. Byington, *Open-Air Preaching*, 9.

open air preaching was scorned by most of the Israelite community, Jeremiah and the other prophets not only continued to preach but had a command from God to do so, as William Evans highlights:

> The sublime evangelical predictions of Isaiah; the mournful dirges of Jeremiah; the symbolical and picturesque visions of Ezekiel— all these, for the most part, were announced in the streets of the great cities of Jerusalem and Babylon. Throughout the streets of Ninevah resounded the warning voice of the prophet Jonah. The message of Micah, Nahum, and the rest of the minor prophets was, without question, "a song of the winds." Nehemiah's great revival sermon was preached in the street of Jerusalem, close to the water-gate (Neh. 8:1, 3).[5]

The places where the prophets preached would have been thronging with people. Their messages were unsavory to most, even though the people were "religious." These men used no tricks or methods. They sought out the people and preached to them, regardless of their relationship with them. They preached the Word of God regardless of the response to their message. They did not concern themselves with earning the people's trust. They knew the message was from God, and they had been told to preach it. It mattered little whether they preached in a busy street or on top of a hill. An audience of strangers or friends made no difference. They knew that the preached Word, not their relationship with the audience, contained the power of God unto salvation. Even postexilic Israel preferred public spaces as the place of proclamation. Ezra commanded the people of Israel to repent as they sat "in the street of the house of God" (Ezra 10:9–14). He preached from a raised outdoor platform and explained the Word of God to the people (Nehemiah 8 and 9 show the same thing). Open air preaching was the evangelism method most preferred by Old Testament preachers.

This never changes in the New Testament either, when cultures become more settled and "sophisticated." Even though open air preaching was no longer the only or even expected method, it was still commonly used by God. In fact, it expands in the New Testament beyond the scope of what we see in the Old. John the Baptist preached

---

5. William Evans, *Open Air Preaching* (New York: Fleming H. Revell, 1901), 4–5.

this way. As a Jew he would have had access to the synagogues, but he decisively chose to stay away from them. The New Testament never suggests that he sought them out, nor does it condemn him for this, recognizing instead that "among those that are born of women there is not a greater prophet than John the Baptist," an open air preacher (Luke 7:28). Jesus Himself preached on mountains, seashores, in the city streets, even on the edge of a well. These men sought out the people and preached to them. Nothing cute or trendy. They simply trusted in the power of the preached Word of God and went out and proclaimed it.

Jesus not only preached in the open but also commissioned the disciples to do so. When they are sent forth to preach the kingdom of heaven, there is no mention of Jesus telling them to make friends or influence people first. He never tells them to preach only in the synagogues. Although they likely shared the gospel in houses, much of the work must have been done outside. And when they were rejected, as Jesus predicted, they are told to shake the dust from their feet and go to another city, preaching again (Matt. 10:14; Luke 9:5–6). He knew they would be mocked. He knew the preaching of the gospel would be a scandal to most. But He says to go forth and do it anyway. In the parable of the marriage feast, we read the lord of the feast say to the servant, "Go out into the highways and hedges, and compel them to come in, that my house may be filled" (Luke 14:23). This is an exemplary sentence for the aim of open air preaching, and it comes from the mouth of our Lord. Christ's disciples were sent out to "compel" the people to "come in."

After Pentecost the disciples went to the streets with their message, which explains the enormous number of new converts piling into the church. Peter proclaimed the Word of God at Solomon's Portico, which would have been outside (Acts 3:11–26). Philip preached on the streets of Samaria (Acts 8:6–8). It is true Paul and others preached in synagogues, but their most memorable seasons came while preaching in the open air. The entire city of Antioch was shaken by Paul's outdoor deliveries (Acts 13:44–52). His first European convert came as a result of open air evangelism (Acts 16:11–15). His address on Mars Hill was in the middle of the city, away from the confines of any synagogue (Acts 17:22–34). When taken into custody by the Roman guards, Paul preached to "men, brethren, and fathers" (Acts 22:1) from the castle stairs as the Jews attempted to mob him. Apollos publicly refuted the Jews on the streets of Achaia (Acts 18:27–28). These few examples alone force us to conclude that open air preaching was the preferred method of spreading the gospel in both the Old and New Testaments.

Jesus left His disciples with the command to go into all the world and preach the gospel, but of course the world is not restricted to those within the church. It also consists of people who have never worshiped inside a church and would never do so unless they were saved. Thus, to preach the gospel to the world, Christ's disciples must go outside the church building to do it. We must "get all we can into the churches, and there preach to them, and then to 'go out into the streets and lanes of the cities, and into the highways and hedges,' and hunt up all the rest, and preach to them also."[6] There was a time in Western culture when most people, including the lost, would come to church. Those days no longer exist. The church must go to the lost. There will always be more lost people outside church walls than within, which is why preaching must also happen wherever the lost may be. The command is not, "Go into all the world and tell people to come to church." Nor is it, "Go into all the world and be good examples to the lost." Nor is the command to build houses or even relationships. All the above are fine things to do. But when it comes to preaching and, more particularly, evangelism, we must never substitute relationships for the gospel. The command is to go into the world and preach the gospel. As Spurgeon illustrates, this is what open air preaching seeks to do: "The great benefit of open-air preaching is that we get so many newcomers to hear the Gospel who otherwise would never hear it. The Gospel command is, 'Go ye into all the world, and preach the gospel to every creature,' but it is so little obeyed that one would imagine that it ran thus, 'Go into your own place of worship and preach the Gospel to the few creatures who will come inside.'"[7] Wherever the lost are gathered, a preacher should always be preaching to them, because "how shall they hear without a preacher?" (Rom. 10:14).

What about examples in church history? Do we see any cessation of open air preaching as the church progresses and becomes more

---

6. William Taylor, *Seven Years' Street Preaching in San Francisco* (London: Forgotten Books, 2015), 18.

7. Spurgeon, *Lectures to My Students*, 275.

established? On the contrary, Spurgeon points out, "It would be very easy to prove revivals of religion have usually been accompanied, if not caused, by a considerable amount of preaching out of doors, or in unusual places."[8] According to the church historian Eusebius, the disciples of the first apostles "everywhere prosecuted the preaching of the gospel, sowing the seeds of heavenly doctrine throughout the whole world."[9] Michael Green says the same thing in his book, *Evangelism in the Early Church*: "The evidence is not as full as we should like, but there can be no doubt that this open air evangelism continued throughout the first two centuries…. Irenaeus was accustomed to preaching in the market places not only of the city of Lugdunum but also of the market towns and villages round about. Cyprian even dared the authorities to arrest him as he preached in the market place during a period of persecution."[10] Green says in another place that the early church "had a penchant for small open air meetings…. It is salutary to recall that the early Christians had no churches during the first two centuries, the time of their major expansion. They had perforce to use the open air."[11]

The same penchant for public evangelism can be seen as the gospel advanced through the centuries. Sometimes this was due to the lack of buildings for Christians to gather in, but more often than not it was simply for the sake of getting the gospel to the lost. In 633, for example, at the dawn of the Middle Ages, King Oswald of Northumbria sent for a bishop named Aldan for the purpose of evangelizing his territory. Church buildings had not yet been established, so Aldan is said to have "entered into evangelization on horseback."[12]

Crowded markets and thoroughfares were always seen as excellent opportunities for proclaiming the gospel. Bernard of Clairvaux (1090–1153) became "a public preacher of considerable distinction" when a group of monks were thrown out of their seclusion and "into

---

8. Spurgeon, *Lectures to My Students*, 275.
9. Spurgeon, *Lectures to My Students*, 274.
10. Michael Green, *Evangelism in the Early Church* (Grand Rapids: Eerdmans, 1970), 304.
11. Green, *Evangelism in the Early Church*, 23.
12. David L. Larsen, *The Company of the Preachers* (Grand Rapids: Kregel Publications, 1998), 110.

the highways and byways of public concourse."[13] He was one of the first monks to bring gospel preaching outside of the cloister. People were milling about the streets, so the monks began to preach.

Arnold of Brescia (1090–1155) is another example. He proclaimed the Word of God to great crowds in Brescia, eventually heading to Rome, where he "denounced papal usurpations at the very gates of the Vatican."[14] Arnold was a monk who became so infuriated by Roman Catholic teachings that he "took his stand in the streets of his native Brescia, and began to thunder forth his scheme of reform."[15] Some time later, the bishop of Brescia "found his entire flock deserting the cathedral and assembling daily in the marketplace, crowing round the eloquent preacher, and listening with applause to his fierce philippies, so that he bestirred himself to silence the courageous monk."[16] Eventually Arnold was burned alive by Roman Catholic authorities.

Interestingly enough, Francis of Assisi (1182–1226), the man traditionally credited with the phrase "Preach the gospel at all times and when necessary use words," is said to have "usually preached out of doors, in the marketplaces, from church steps, from the walls of castle courtyards."[17] Although we vehemently disagree with the doctrine these men preached, they show us that open air preaching has always been a valuable means for getting the gospel to the lost, even before the Reformation.

The Protestant Reformation came about in large part through publicly preaching the gospel. Henry of Lausanne in the twelfth century is reported to have preached against transubstantiation on the streets. John Wycliffe, the "morning star" of the Reformation, was the figurehead of a group in England who regularly preached against Roman Catholicism in the open air.[18] This kind of evangelism led the way for the men we now call the Reformers. John Knox began his ministry as

13. Larsen, *Company of the Preachers*, 111.

14. Spurgeon, *Lectures to My Students*, 275.

15. J. A. Wylie, *The History of Protestantism*, vol. 1 (London: Cassell & Company, 1880), 52.

16. Wylie, *History of Protestantism*, 1:52.

17. EWTN, "St. Francis of Assisi: Founder of the Franciscan Order," accessed May 25, 2018, http://www.ewtn.com/saintsHoly/saints/F/stfrancisofassisi.asp.

18. James Gairdner, *Lollardy and the Reformation in England: An Historical Survey*, vol. 2 (London: Macmillan, 1908), 47.

a bodyguard for a street preacher. When the preacher was martyred, Knox regularly preached "faith alone by grace alone in Christ alone" in the same manner as his predecessor.[19] Without open air preaching, the Protestant faith might have been much slower in its break from Roman Catholicism. One could even ask, as Spurgeon does, whether the Reformation would have come about at all if not for this kind of preaching: "Where would the Reformation have been if its great preachers had confined themselves to churches and cathedrals? How would the common people have become indoctrinated with the Gospel had it not been for those far-wandering evangelists, the colporteurs, and those daring innovators who found a pulpit on every heap of stones, and an audience chamber in every open space near the abodes of men?"[20]

Every generation of the church seems to have had men preaching in this way. John Bunyan, George Whitefield, John Wesley, and Charles Spurgeon regularly did so. George Whitefield said, "I never was more acceptable to my Master than when I was standing to teach those hearers in the open fields."[21] Elsewhere he said, "I now preach to ten times more people than I should, if I had been confined to the Churches."[22] John Wesley recorded, "I am well assured I did far more good to my Lincolnshire parishioners by preaching three days on my father's tomb than I did by preaching three years in his pulpit."[23] Elsewhere he admitted, "To this day field preaching is a cross to me, but I know my commission and see no other way of preaching the gospel to every creature."[24] It could be argued that the eighteenth-century Welsh Revival came about through the open air preaching of Daniel Rowland, Howell Harris, and others.[25] Another revival in India came in part through the work of William

---

19. Gervase N. Charmley, "John Knox: The Making of a Reformer," *Banner of Truth*, October 21, 2015, https://banneroftruth.org/us/resources/articles/2015/john-knox-the-making-of-a-reformer/.

20. Spurgeon, *Lectures to My Students*, 254.

21. Arnold Dallimore, *George Whitfield: God's Anointed Servant* (Wheaton, Ill.: Crossway, 1990), 46.

22. Arnold Dallimore, *George Whitefield: The Life and Times of the Great Evangelist of the Eighteenth-Century Revival*, vol. 1 (Carlisle, Pa.: Banner of Truth, 1970), 61.

23. Dallimore, *George Whitefield: The Life and Times*, 1:122.

24. Dallimore, *George Whitefield: The Life and Times*, 1:221.

25. See especially both volumes of John Morgan Jones and William Morgan, *The Calvinistic Methodist Fathers of Wales* (1890; repr., Carlisle, Pa.: Banner of Truth, 2016).

Carey.[26] Robert Flockhart was one convert of Carey's ministry who, upon returning to Scotland, preached publicly for four decades.[27] Horatius Bonar notes how God blessed these men for their outdoor preaching: "They preached and labored in season and out of season, in churches, barns, schoolhouses, streets, or highways, to deal faithfully and closely with men's consciences wherever they may happen to be brought into contact with them.... This is to turn the world upside down, to offend every rule of good breeding, and to tear up the landmarks of civilized society.... *This has ever been one of the great secrets of success.*"[28]

In modern times, D. L. Moody, Leonard Ravenhill, Paul Washer, Albert N. Martin, Rob Ventura, and even Westminster Theological Seminary professor Cornelius Van Til were all open air preachers. Today it is possible to find people preaching openly in every major city in North America and Western Europe, and a smattering of others in South America, India, and other "hard to reach" areas. It seems conclusive to say that God has always used open air proclamation as a means for getting the gospel to the lost.

---

26. Edward Glinney, ed., *Missions in a New Millennium* (Grand Rapids: Kregel Publications, 2000), 301.

27. Robert Flockhart, *The Street Preacher* (Grand Rapids: Baker, 1977), 185–208.

28. Horatius Bonar, *True Revival* (Pensacola, Fla.: Chapel Library, 2000), 11 (emphasis added).

## Questions

1. How could studying the Scriptures and church history help the
   preacher before he goes to the streets?

2. How would you respond to someone who says that open air preaching does not work anymore?

3. What are the best ways to challenge "seeker-friendly" and "friendship
   evangelism" cultures to consider open air preaching?

# Chapter Two

# Theology for Open Air Preaching

*One often hears it said that the heathen are hungering and thirsting for the gospel. That statement is far too sweeping to be acceptable.*
—R. B. Kuiper, *God-Centered Evangelism*

It is one thing to know that open air preaching should be done—it is another to do it properly. A. W. Tozer said, "What comes into our minds when we think about God is the most important thing about us."[1] It is also the most important thing about our approach to preaching. A minister's view of God and the gospel will influence the way he preaches. Someone who believes that God saves irrespective of a person's cooperation or choice will go about his work much differently than someone who holds that God and man have a mutual part in salvation. Both camps can be found preaching today, but we believe that only one can be doing the work correctly. The position we will take in this book is unapologetically monergistic, or the belief that "salvation is of the LORD" (Jonah 2:9; Ps. 3:8) and is the result of divine election from before the foundation of the world, without any foreseen merit in the one elected.

## The Importance of a Correct View of God
Before we proceed, however, there needs to be a word of caution. A preacher needs to embrace proper theology, as we will point out, but

---

1. A. W. Tozer, *The Knowledge of the Holy* (New York: Harper & Row, 1961), 1.

more than anything else he must have a constant sense of the glory and majesty of God, along with a real sense of the Holy Spirit in his life. Without being gripped by these realities, he will not be able to stay in the trenches on a regular basis, nor will he preach in a proper manner. Men like Ravenhill and Wesley disagreed with the theology we will put forward, yet they were used by God and persevered for many years despite opposition. A deep love for the Lord, a deep love for men, dependence on the Holy Spirit, and a biblical view of conversion are things as much required as anything else discussed in this chapter. Otherwise a preacher is nothing more than "sounding brass, or a tinkling cymbal" (1 Cor. 13:1).[2]

First of all, Scripture is clear that the gospel is "the power of God unto salvation to every one that believeth" (Rom. 1:16). God's chosen method of evangelism is the gospel. Someone's moral behavior has no power to save. Nor do soup kitchens or money or friendships. The Scriptures declare that God saves through the gospel. We know many atheists and Muslims who would provide a decent enough example for how one should live, if you simply mean being nice or loving. We know many Roman Catholics who would feed an entire city or spend years in front of an abortion mill if given the chance. But the lost do not need our good example to be saved. As Christians we are called to be holy as Christ is holy and to love our neighbor as ourselves. But soup kitchens and friendships do not have the power to save. What people need more than anything else is for someone to share the gospel with them. The ears of the lost need to be filled with the gospel of Christ, as William Taylor emphasizes: "The whole matter resolves itself into this, that these ten millions of our neighbors, whom we are commanded to love as we love ourselves, must have 'the gospel preached to them,' or the mass of them will go to perdition. They are blinded by the god of this world, and will not come to us. Should we not, in the name and spirit of Him who came to seek and to save the lost, 'go' to them?"[3]

Paul says later in Romans, "So then faith cometh by hearing, and hearing by the word of God" (Rom. 10:17). This method of hearing the

---

2. We are grateful to our friend Charles Leiter for pointing this out to us. Much of the language here is his.

3. Taylor, *Seven Years' Street Preaching*, 20.

gospel is repeated throughout his letters: "For this cause also thank we God without ceasing, because, when ye received the word of God which ye heard of us, ye received it not as the word of men, but as it is in truth, the word of God, which effectually worketh also in you that believe" (1 Thess. 2:13); "Received ye the Spirit by the works of the law, or by the hearing of faith?" (Gal. 3:2); "In whom ye also trusted, after that ye heard the word of truth, the gospel of your salvation" (Eph. 1:13). Even Peter says it was those "that have preached the gospel unto you with the Holy Ghost sent down from heaven" (1 Peter 1:12) that caused the glories of Christ to be made known, not the behavior or example of the preachers. This is where the role of the open air preacher comes in: "How then shall they call on him in whom they have not believed? and how shall they believe in him of whom they have not heard? and how shall they hear without a preacher?" (Rom. 10:14). Biblical evangelism is simply getting the gospel to the lost. Nothing cute or clever.

Many preachers claim to believe what Paul says about the power of the gospel to save, but when it comes to evangelism you will rarely see them living this out. They will pray for hoards of people without ever sharing the gospel with them. They will fly thousands of miles to build someone a house, trying to share the gospel by their deeds. But that is not what we find in the Scriptures. Biblical evangelism is getting the gospel into people's ears, which requires us to use our mouths, not our behavior. Although our behavior must be consistent with what we are preaching, it is the Holy Spirit working through the gospel of Christ, never our behavior, that saves. This is why people must hear the gospel. Any method that demotes the gospel beneath some other trick or scheme is a lack of faith in the gospel, which alone contains the "power of God" to save (Rom. 1:16).

Al Baker has also noticed this tendency to evangelize with clever schemes instead of the gospel: "Many of the leading pastors of our day reject out of hand direct, intentional, bold evangelistic outreach. They tend to over-contextualize the gospel message when in the midst of atheist, agnostics, and militant unbelievers.... And what's behind this approach is the convinced position by many that direct, bold, intentional, Scripture-saturated evangelism simply does not work in our postmodern world."[4]

## The Importance of a Correct View of Man

Tozer's saying about what comes into our minds when we think about God is also true about the preacher's view of man. A wrong view of man will cause a wrong approach to the task. What is man? Is he radically depraved or not? Is there anything in him that desires God prior to his regeneration? Is man capable of choosing God based on his own free decision? It would be wrong to say that the preacher's view of man is subordinate to his view of God. It would also be wrong to say that his view of God is subordinate to his view of man. They go together. Without a right view of God, a preacher cannot have a right view of man; without a right view of man, he cannot have a right view of God. Jesus "knew what was in man" (John 2:25). To be a proper ambassador of Jesus Christ, we must strive to do the same.

The Bible does not teach that men are merely sick or feeble—they are dead in sin (Eph. 2:1). Adam died spiritually the day he ate the forbidden fruit (Gen. 2:17). His death shifted his view of God and caused him to be terrified. After Adam ate the fruit, he did not come running out of the trees whenever God came looking for him. Adam was hiding. His heart must have pounded with dread. His sin caused a separation between him and God, and it has been so ever since for every child of Adam: "And God saw that the wickedness of man was great in the earth, and that every imagination of the thoughts of his heart was only evil continually" (Gen. 6:5). Rather than seeking God, "the soul of the wicked desireth evil" (Prov. 21:10). Rather than communing with God, Adam was exiled from paradise. His firstborn child would turn out to be a murderer. The Bible does not teach that man's will is merely inclined to do evil. It teaches that men are enslaved to do evil (John 8:34). The natural man has been blinded by the "god of this world" (2 Cor. 4:4), and his chief desire is to dethrone God.

---

4. Al Baker, "Three Reasons Why We Need Evangelists," Banner of Truth, October 23, 2017, https://banneroftruth.org/us/resources/articles/2017/three-reasons-need-evangelists/?utm_content=bufferb6c11&utm_medium=social&utm_source=facebook.com&utm_campaign=buffer.

The Bible also teaches that men's hearts are "deceitful above all things, and desperately wicked" (Jer. 17:9) and that lost men live "in the lusts of [their] flesh, fulfilling the desires of the flesh and of the mind" and are "by nature the children of wrath" (Eph. 2:3). A person like this could never choose God, nor is there any notion of libertarian free will in the Scriptures. Consider again, "For every one that doeth evil hateth the light, neither cometh to the light, lest his deeds should be reproved" (John 3:20). Just as a criminal will not seek the police, an unregenerate man will not seek God. He knows that his deeds are evil and that God is a righteous judge. No one would ever come to God by his own free will, because all men apart from regeneration are dead and shackled to sin. They are not free to cease from sinning. But it is worse than this. Unregenerate men hate God. They are "enemies in [their] mind" toward God (Col. 1:21). Why would anyone assume that people who hate God would willingly come to Him apart from a miracle? "The wicked are estranged from the womb: they go astray as soon as they be born, speaking lies" (Ps. 58:3). Birds are born with the instinct to fly. Plants have the instinct to seek the sun. Fish have an inborn desire to swim. Man is born with a homicidal passion to destroy God and his neighbor for the sake of advancing his own kingdom: "The LORD said in his heart, I will not again curse the ground any more for man's sake; for the imagination of man's heart is evil from his youth" (Gen. 8:21).

Unregenerate man could even be considered deranged. Sin has caused him to live and move upside down. Made for the Creator, he lives for the creature (Rom. 1:18–25). Made to worship God, he would rather spend his life worshiping the earth. When Adam fell, we all fell with him: "In Adam all die" (1 Cor. 15:22) and "by one man's disobedience many were made sinners" (Rom. 5:19). This is the way of man: haters of God (Rom. 1:30) and dead in sin (Eph. 2:1). These are the people whom the preacher is trying to reach. Sin courses through their veins as water does a brook. They gulp in sin like air. You cannot manipulate a man like this to come to life. A dead man never chooses to start breathing again, nor could he. A man who hates God will never choose to love Him. Consider the story of Joseph. His brothers "hated him" (Gen. 37:4–5, 8) so much that they "could not speak peaceably unto him" (Gen. 37:4). This is what a preacher encounters any time he goes out with the gospel. This is why it is absurd to think that an unregenerate man would choose to speak friendly words about God, much less worship and submit to Him.

If this is the condition of man, what chance do we have as open air preachers? What can we do for people who are dead? The answer is nothing, unless God moves. Ezekiel was shown a pile of dry bones in a valley and asked by the Lord if they could live. He did not say yes or no but rather, "O Lord GOD, thou knowest." This is the proper response when it comes to raising dead men to life. If the Lord wills it, it will be so. If He does not, it will not be. The preacher plants and waters, but "God…giveth the increase" (1 Cor. 3:7). Consider John Owen's thoughts on the subject: "Satan's original great design, wherever the gospel is preached, is to blind the eyes of men, that the light of the glorious gospel of Christ, who is the image of God, should not shine unto them…. He blinds the minds of the most, that they shall not behold any thing of the glory of Christ therein. By this means he continues his rule in the children of disobedience. *With respect unto the elect, God overpowers him herein.*"[5]

This is foundational for evangelism. Even though we are called to go into the world and preach, we must remember that "a man can receive nothing, except it be given him from heaven" (John 3:27). Men will never choose God, regardless of how eloquently we preach or how attractive our gimmicks. The only chance men have is if God has mercy on them. He must "rend the heavens…[and] come down" (Isa. 64:1). The goal of preaching is to get the gospel to the people, not to save them, since salvation is of the Lord, not the preacher: "God never laid it upon thee to convert those he sends thee to. No, to publish the gospel is thy duty."[6] This is why anything cute or silly or wise according to this world will only distract from the simple message of the cross. Proclaiming the gospel must be the preacher's goal.

---

5. John Owen, *The Glory of Christ* (1850; repr., Carlisle, Pa.: Banner of Truth, 1965), 404 (emphasis added).

6. William Gurnall, *The Christian in Complete Armour* (1662; repr., London: Banner of Truth, 1964), 574.

## The Advantages of God's Unconditional Election and Man's Radical Depravity

God's unconditional election is a great comfort to the preacher since it is not up to him to save sinners—"No man can come to me, except the Father which hath sent me draw him" (John 6:44). This is why a preacher does not rely on props or tricks. He does not need to use "shock and awe" or "bait and switch" tactics. The only instruments he needs are intercessory prayer and the gospel. Open air preaching is not about producing converts but rather delivering the gospel faithfully: "Evangelism is man's work, but the giving of faith is God's."[7] This is crucial to understand. If a preacher believes that salvation is up to him instead of the Lord, then whenever he is not seeing converts he will be tempted to manipulate the crowd or rely on worldly wisdom. He will either water down the gospel or become harsh and grating.

If God is sovereign in salvation and man is incapable of being born again apart from His regenerating grace, then the preacher can go out in total dependence on God. He will be liberated from the burden of saying the right thing or the fear of saying the wrong thing or "pushing people further away" from God. People whose minds are set on the flesh are hostile to God and can scarcely be pushed much further than they already are (Rom. 8:7). This allows the preacher to focus on proclaiming the gospel instead of using his own devices. We know several men who have come to believe the truths of Reformed theology through their evangelism work. They realize after preaching for a while that only God can save people who are "full of evil, and madness is in their heart while they live" (Eccl. 9:3). Only God can replace "the stony heart" with a "heart of flesh" (Ezek. 36:26). Only God can cause the scales of the blind to fall so they can see the beauty of the Son.

Belief in God's sovereignty and the radical depravity of man should also keep the open air preacher humble. It will never be his "wisdom of words" that saves or attracts sinners to Jesus Christ (1 Cor. 1:17). A preacher must avoid assuming he has anything to do with someone's salvation apart from sharing the gospel. The work is too important. Unsaved people are dead. This should motivate the preacher to be

---

7. J. I. Packer, *Evangelism and the Sovereignty of God* (Nottingham, England: Inter-Varsity Press, 2008), 45.

constant in prayer and to be a vessel set apart as holy, "meet for the master's use" (2 Tim. 2:21). He must remember that he is preaching to dead bones and that "the wicked, through the pride of his countenance, will not seek after God: God is not in all his thoughts" (Ps. 10:4). Without this understanding, the preacher will try to entice the person's emotions in unbiblical ways. He will attempt to speak cleverly, which is exactly the opposite of Paul, who was "rude in speech" (2 Cor. 11:6).

This does not mean a preacher should not study to show himself "approved" (2 Tim. 2:15). Nor should he be sloppy or uncouth in his delivery of the gospel. Embracing the doctrines of God's sovereignty and man's depravity means that he will be kept from two equally poisonous mind-sets. The first one is discouragement. Faithful preachers have rightly pointed out that were it not for the sovereignty of God in salvation, they would have quit the ministry long ago: "Faith in the sovereignty of God's government and grace is the only thing that can sustain it, for it is the only thing that can give us the resilience that we need if we are to evangelize boldly and persistently, and not be daunted by temporary setbacks. So far from being weakened by this faith, therefore, evangelism will inevitably be weak and lack staying power without it."[8]

If there is ever a ministry where staying power is needed, it is open air preaching. From the perspective of "things seen," it can be some of the most unrewarding work there is. Knowing that God is sovereign will oftentimes be the only comfort a preacher will have. William Evans gives us an example from 1901:

> The results of open air work are, for the most part, never known to the workers. The present Bishop of Liverpool was converted while listening to a talk given at an open air meeting. He does not know the name of the man who spoke the word of life that night, and the man who spoke the word does not know that it touched the Bishop's heart and was the means of leading him to Christ. That preacher might have gone home that night and said to himself: "Well, what is the use of preaching in the open air anyway? Nobody seems to be converted. I see no results of my work."[9]

---

8. Packer, *Evangelism and the Sovereignty of God*, 44.
9. Evans, *Open Air Preaching*, 24.

Preaching the gospel glorifies the Lord, regardless of "results." And is this not enough? The Lord is glorified every time we preach the cross, and every time we preach we are being obedient to His command. Evans reminds us to "preach the Word in faith and power. That, and that alone, is our duty; leave the results with God. If it is wise to let you see them He will do it; if you do not see them as you would like to, still plod on."[10]

Belief in God's unconditional election and man's radical depravity will also keep the preacher from becoming proud. Any tangible fruit or salvific success from his work will not be attributed to him, since salvation "is not of him that willeth, nor of him that runneth, but of God that sheweth mercy" (Rom. 9:16). If the preacher sees bones rattle to life, he will know he was preaching to dead men. He will know it is no credit of his that some were raised to "newness of life" (Rom. 6:4). He will glorify God, not his own preaching, since it was God who was "sought of them that asked not for me; I am found of them that sought me not" (Isa. 65:1).

## A Synergist Should Not Be Engaging in Open Air Preaching

We believe that a synergist, or one who believes salvation is a cooperative effort between God and man, has no business evangelizing. A statement like this will be unsettling for some, but any position other than monergism, or the view that God alone saves irrespective of a person's choice or decision, tends to detract from God's glory and lead to pride and numerous false conversions. A synergist is always obligated to do all he can to manipulate the will of man into "choosing" God. This kind of evangelism attempts to attract men with trendy methods or smooth words rather than the gospel.[11] The notion of libertarian free will as it pertains to salvation is essentially in the same family as the Roman Catholic works-based system. It says, "Christ has done His part, now you must do yours. Christ did a little, now you do a little." But if a person has to choose Christ in order to be saved, what does this entail? Walking

---

10. Evans, *Open Air Preaching*, 25.

11. Sadly, even many Reformed ministers adopt the same pragmatic approaches to evangelism and church practices as synergists. It is usually the result of either a lack of faith in the power of the gospel to save sinners or fear of man's reaction to the offense of the gospel.

an aisle? Saying a prayer? Raising a hand? Getting baptized? Anything the synergist puts forward will by default make it works-based.

On the contrary, the Bible shows that man is saved because God gives him a new heart, and in response man repents and believes the gospel. God raises the spiritually dead to life. He loosens the constraints of sin. The person becomes a new creation with a new principle of life. Question 73 of the Westminster Larger Catechism asks, "How does faith justify a sinner in the sight of God?" To which it answers, "Not because of those other graces which do always accompany it, or of good works that are the fruits of it, nor as if the grace of faith, or any act thereof, were imputed to him for his justification; but only as it is an instrument by which he receives and applies Christ and his righteousness."

The only choice when it comes to salvation belongs to God, and rightly so. Christ prayed asking that His Father's will be done, not man's, because man's will is undone. Synergism is man-worshiping and unbiblical, and anyone who denies God's sovereignty in predestinating some persons to be saved is a synergist. While the monergist gives all glory to God, the synergist gives some of His glory to man since it is man who "chooses."

But of course we must preach to all the world, declaring that "all men every where" should repent (Acts 17:30). The open air preacher must never be hyper-Calvinistic. We must wrestle with men's souls, pleading that they be reconciled to God through Jesus Christ (2 Cor. 5:20). We must tell men to "choose you this day whom ye will serve" (Josh. 24:15), though the effectual call of the gospel is God's work alone. He is sovereign in all things, especially salvation, even though He condescends to use "the foolishness of preaching to save them that believe" (1 Cor. 1:21). Our war cry must be the gospel. We must preach the cross. We must preach repentance and faith in Christ, bidding sinners to come to Him, knowing all the while that salvation is a gift of God: "Can the Ethiopian change his skin, or the leopard his spots? then may ye also do good, that are accustomed to do evil" (Jer. 13:23). The open air preacher's method is getting the Word of God to the people, whether at a college campus, downtown, an abortion clinic, or in front of a sports stadium. What happens next is up to God.

## Questions

1. When it comes to open air preaching, how would the synergist's approach differ from the monergist's, and why does it matter?

2. How would you approach an open air preacher who is a synergist? Would you preach with him? Why or why not?

3. Do you agree that anything other than a monergistic view of salvation is unbiblical? Do you believe that regeneration logically precedes saving faith?

# Chapter Three

# The Local Church and the Open Air Preacher

*Unto this catholic visible church Christ hath given the ministry, oracles, and ordinances of God, for the gathering and perfecting of the saints, in this life, to the end of the world.*
—The Westminster Confession of Faith 25.3

The relationship between open air preachers and the local church has always been complicated. Even in Scripture the religious community seems bewildered whenever it comes to dealing with this kind of preacher. On the surface it would seem that church leadership and preachers would love to work together. Many Reformed open air preachers rightly seek to be active members in their local church. An ideal situation would be believers regularly praying for and supporting such a ministry. Likewise, one would think local churches would love to have such a preacher in their congregation. The thought of having a regular evangelist in the community seems great for the church and its outreach. Then why is it so rare to find a healthy, genuine relationship between the evangelist and his local church? Why is this relationship often strained? Does the problem generally come from the preacher or the local church? Can these difficulties be resolved?

## The Open Air Preacher Should Be Active in a Local Church
We believe that a man should be active in his local church if he is going to be preaching on the streets. This should be the general rule, although it may look differently according to each case and circumstance.

Furthermore, a preacher should be approved by his local church or denomination if he is going to preach on the streets. Again, each church or denomination will go about this differently, and this may not always be possible, but this should be the mind-set of the Reformed evangelist.

A preacher must not be a nomad when it comes to the local church. He should be committed to serving and equipping his local body through his ministry on the streets (Eph. 4:11–16). It is easy for him to have a nomadic mind-set because of criticism or lack of support from within the church. He may become discouraged or even embittered as a result. But he must remember that the local church is Christ's bride and should be cherished accordingly. To be active in ministry without any accountability to a local church is dangerous and unbiblical. Everyone has blind spots, including preachers. When Paul was doing ministry in strange lands, he always reverted to the Jerusalem Council whenever a sticky question came up. What is more, he always submitted to its decision. He also returned regularly to Antioch, his sending church, and was in constant communication with the churches and the co-laborers within the communities where he preached. As easy as it is for a preacher to get whisked away into a nomadic ministry, he must do all he can to avoid it. The local church can also provide insight into the workings of the Spirit, locating and suggesting areas where ministry could be useful, again showing that an open air ministry under the oversight of the local church can be extremely useful when done in the right way.

## Qualifications for Open Air Preaching

Who qualifies to be an open air preacher? Some ministers and denominations claim preaching and teaching should be limited only to ordained clergy, whether inside or outside the church. Others, such as 1689 Confessional Baptists, point to the rule of the "Gifted Brethren," covered in chapter 26, paragraph 11 of the 1689 London Baptist Confession: "Although it be incumbent on the bishops or pastors of the churches, to be instant in preaching the word, by way of office, yet the work of preaching the word is not so peculiarly confined to them but that others also gifted and fitted by the Holy Spirit for it, and approved and called by the church, may and ought to perform it." In other words, the church can call and approve certain men to preach the gospel in public without ordaining them to the clergy.

Some ministers and denominations feel that anyone can preach Christ in public since Jesus Himself says, "Go ye into all the world, and preach the gospel to every creature" (Mark 16:15). We would disagree with this, acknowledging a difference between preaching and sharing the gospel. All Christians should actively share the gospel with the lost, but only persons called and sent to preach should do so. Each church and denomination will go about this differently, but as a general principle we believe the open air preacher should be sent out by the local church. At the same time, we believe the local church should willingly and actively examine and train men to preach in public.

In addressing such a complicated issue, it may be beneficial to remember that the idea of a clergyman as some kind of distinguished, religious professional is not necessarily biblical. This is not to deny that the Lord calls men to be pastors or elders of His church. Of course He does, and their authority should therefore be respected. But the whole notion of some "holy man" as distinguished from the "common" Christian is foreign to the Scriptures and the early church. The elder or overseer is simply one of the saints who has been called to direct or oversee the Lord's church and His people. Anything else leans toward religious superstition. Likewise, the idea that only professional clergymen should be allowed to proclaim the gospel in public is not necessarily biblical. It is correct that the church, including pastors or elders, will be necessary when it comes to acknowledging and aiding a man's call to proclaim the gospel. It is also correct that the church should be able to send men and hold others back as they see fit. But the idea that only ordained clergy should be allowed to proclaim the gospel in the open is unfounded. That does not mean there are not qualifications for those who herald the gospel publicly. The Bible is filled with them. But it also does not mean that all evangelists will or should be "ordained" to the work of the clergy, just as not all ordained clergy are called to preaching in the streets.

We believe that only men are called to proclaim the gospel in the open air (1 Tim. 2:12–15) and that they must fit the qualifications of an elder as laid out in 1 Timothy 3 and Titus 1. These are descriptions of a mature follower of Christ. Not all who fit these descriptions will be elders or overseers of a congregation. Likewise, not everyone who fits these descriptions will be an evangelist. But a man should possess the characteristics outlined in these chapters if he is going to be heralding the gospel on the streets. This, again, is why the local church is so important when it comes to open air preaching. It helps assess the preacher's qualifications, but even here there needs to be a word of caution. Some local churches have been known to scrupulously nitpick a preacher's character or ability for the sake of keeping him off the streets. This kind of approach is uncharitable and hindering. Likewise, some preachers have been unfairly critical of their church whenever the leaders offer criticism, rebuke, cautions, or concerns, which is likewise insubordinate and disrespectful to the office entrusted to these leaders by the Lord.

## Resolving Conflict between the Local Church and Open Air Preachers

Sadly, the evangelist might face ostracism from his local church for his activity on the streets. Or maybe the preacher's pastor or elder who supports open air preaching is replaced by one who is against it, leaving the preacher in a difficult spot. Should he stop preaching in such a case? Should he leave his church? We would encourage him in such a situation to meet with the new leadership and gently reason with them from the Scriptures regarding the validity of open air ministry. If the problem cannot be resolved, the preacher should either stop preaching in obedience to his leadership or find another church. At times he will relocate to another city and must spend time finding a church. In other cases his church may dissolve or split. Again, we believe that a preacher should be approved and sent out by his local church, but scenarios do come up when such demands become more complicated. Overall, he should maintain a high view of the church along with a spirit of reasonableness and humility. Likewise, the elders or pastors should seek to maintain a spirit of patience and gratitude toward the preacher, seeking to equip him for the work he has been called to do.

We are not ignorant of the challenges of maintaining a good relationship between the local church and evangelists, even in churches that are healthy. Historically there seems to be a tendency for the local church to shun or criticize these preachers, oftentimes coming from the leadership. Likewise, preachers have tended to shun and criticize the local church, especially the leadership. Where do such tendencies come from? How can they be resolved? We believe that at least three principal reasons are responsible for the conflict. These are not exhaustive, though they are common. These reasons do not justify either the evangelist or the local church in criticizing the other. But perhaps if we put a finger on the sources of conflict it will help avoid such dissension.

First, many local churches, including Reformed churches, are cold and ossified in matters of evangelism. Their members are comfortable in their non-evangelism, and sharing the gospel to the lost as a church would be a strange novelty. They are stuck in the general routines of work, family, church, and sleep. They might diligently attend prayer meetings and Bible studies. But the thought of serving the Lord outside church walls, especially sharing the gospel with strangers, seems odious. Whenever someone is doing evangelism and challenging others to do the same, congregants in general may feel convicted for not doing it. They may also feel threatened. To be challenged to do something other than the normal routine may appear offensive, and usually the one active in evangelism and challenging others to join will be the one to blame. But church members will not always say this aloud. To vocalize such an opinion would be to betray their dislike for evangelism, which would be the same as betraying their dislike for the Savior since evangelism is a direct command from Him. In such a case, they will either avoid the preacher or criticize him on some other front. The reaction will be passive-aggressive. They may try to stop his call to evangelize by attacking his character or preaching style or something else. They may say the preacher will bring a bad reputation to the church, which gives them an excuse to refrain from sharing the gospel with strangers. This kind of response can come from the laymen as well as from pastors and elders.

Second, there is the problem of discomfort caused by open air preaching. Many in the local church, if pressed, would never approve of it. Most have been immersed in a church culture that is seeker-friendly, tolerant of sin, and terrified of offending anyone. Even born-again members of biblical churches have been influenced by the watered-down evangelicalism of our day. Many have been taught that forming friendships and building houses is the best way to evangelize, and they view open air preaching as too brash or cutting. This is a typical reaction of a church culture steeped in unbiblical methods of evangelism. Some in the church may come out a few times with the preacher, excited to join the work, but typically when exposed to the tension of preaching on the streets, these people decide it is not for them. Moreover, some of them will decide it is not for the lost either. When exposed to the depravity of man and the response unbelievers show toward the preaching of the cross, they not only will never participate again but will express concern about any Christian going into the public square and preaching God's truth boldly. Many in the local church believe not only that open air preaching is the wrong way to evangelize but also that it is harmful. They will point to the lack of fruit or the impropriety of raising the voice for Christ. The local church is often embarrassed by these preachers.

Third, the church leadership often shows little support for open air preaching. If the evangelist does not have the backing of his church leaders, he will soon be pressed into a corner and ostracized by the whole body. The leadership's response toward the preacher will be reflected by the congregation. Pastors and elders do not have to openly denounce the work of open air preaching to show their disapproval of it. If they aim to be biblical, they will know they could not openly denounce it. To do so would be to denounce the Bible. But leaders can show disapproval of public evangelism by their actions or lack thereof. If they do not encourage the body to support the preacher, join him on the streets, or at the very least publicly pray for him, then neither will the church. The leadership also may feel intimidated by his zeal and courage. This is not to puff up the preacher—he should know that any courage he has comes from the Lord, not himself—but the leadership may fear that the congregation will see them as less zealous because they do not join the street work, which can create friction between the church and the preacher.

Fourth, the church leadership may regard preaching on the streets as "easy" or a kind of lesser ministry compared to preaching from the pulpit, feeding the flock, and making home visits. Pastors and church members have been heard referring to open air work as "playing around," and while most would not openly say such a thing, many feel the same way. The preacher should show patience to such reactions while at the same time encouraging the critics of this sort to join him one day on the streets. Anyone who has participated in this ministry, whether preaching or coming alongside one who does, is usually astonished by how taxing it is. The preacher is frequently besieged by attacks from unbelievers, "believers," police officers, heat or cold or wind or rain, thirst and hunger, and the fatigue of standing on your feet for long hours, not to mention the demands on the emotions and vocal cords.

There is also the common, unhealthy scenario of the open air preacher doing nearly all of the church's evangelism. The church merely relegates the public proclamation of the gospel to the preacher and assumes it has done its evangelism duties. Ideally there will be a healthy interaction between the street preacher's evangelism and that done by the rest of the congregation. Churches can support the preacher by having a team of people praying for him, by joining him to hand out gospel tracts and engaging in evangelistic conversation, or even in giving monetarily to cover living expenses or evangelistic resources like tracts or voice amplifiers. Likewise, the preacher could help the church by coming alongside brothers and sisters who want to do more evangelism but are not as seasoned.

**The Open Air Preacher Should Be an Exemplary Churchman**
Despite the history of tense relationships between the open air preacher and the local church, the most important thing for the preacher is to be active in his local church. He should be an exemplary churchman. Not only does Christ require this but there are pastors, elders, and local bodies who would love to encourage and support these preachers. Many already do. The evangelist must extend the same grace and patience toward his local body that he expects from them. The best thing he can do is to "have compassion on the ignorant, and on them that are out of the way; for that he himself also is compassed with infirmity" (Heb. 5:2). Perhaps he can lead his church and its leaders to see the beauty of such a biblical approach to evangelism. Churches are imperfect because they are made up of imperfect people, including the preacher. He must remember that he also has not yet attained the goal. We are all in the process of progressive sanctification, becoming more like Christ. The

street preacher needs to be even more charitable and gentle within his church than he is when preaching to the lost outside of it. John Calvin addressed an issue common with preachers who, sensing coldness or hostility toward them, decide they must leave their church at once, without attempting to allay the problem:

> In bearing with imperfections of life we ought to be far more considerate…. For there have always been those who, imbued with a false conviction of their own perfect sanctity, as if they had already become a sort of airy spirits, spurned association with all men in whom they discern any remnant of human nature…. For where the Lord requires kindness, they neglect it and give themselves over completely to immoderate severity. Indeed, because they think no church exists where there are not perfect purity and integrity of life, they depart out of hatred of wickedness from the lawful church, while they fancy themselves turning aside from the faction of the wicked.[1]

Remember that many ministers and churches are unfamiliar with open air preaching. A preacher can help equip the saints "for the work of the ministry" by providing members with a better knowledge of open air preaching and the ways it can be used by the church (Eph. 4:12). For example, many Christians are shy. They would love to share their faith but are afraid or unsure about how to do it. As any evangelist knows, simply coming out while he proclaims the gospel creates ample opportunities for sharing the faith and, if nothing else, handing out gospel tracts or praying. We have met several people who got over their fears of witnessing by going out with a preacher on a regular basis. Such preaching is a lightning rod for evangelistic encounters. It makes one-on-one witnessing easier because the topic of Christ is already "in the air."

The local church can support its open air preacher by making sure he has not only a constant supply of tracts, laborers, and financial support when available but also a group of prayer warriors who commit time each week to pray for him. Even if the church lacks financial support, it should not lack people to aid his preaching. Assigning a couple

---

1. John Calvin, *Institutes of the Christian Religion*, ed. John McNeill (Louisville, Ky.: Westminster Press, 1960), 4.1.13.

of members each week to go out with the preacher would do wonders not only for the preacher but for the cause of Christ within the church. The benefits that come from going out and sharing Christ are immense. If the entire church were involved in such a ministry, it would soon have a fire to share the gospel not only outdoors but at their places of work and with family members. Sharing the gospel is infectious. Once you do it on the streets, whether through preaching or conversation, it is much easier to do everywhere else.

Going to the streets with the gospel also helps the church to become more realistic about what it faces in the world today. When we keep the gospel within the church, it is easy to have the mind-set that most people love Christ or, at best, do not hate Him. A few days on the streets will remove many unbiblical notions. This in turn will cause the church to be more zealous in prayer and to see the truths of the Bible more clearly, especially as it concerns men being "dead in trespasses and sins" (Eph. 2:1) and at "enmity against God" (Rom. 8:7). The church and the open air preacher need one another. A preacher must commit himself to being a reliable, patient churchman. He must be the one to address any problem or tension that exists between his ministry and the local church. He must never be a lone wolf or a nomad.

## Questions

1. What are some steps an open air preacher can take to facilitate a healthy relationship with his church?

2. How can a preacher motivate other church members to join him on the streets?

3. Are there ever circumstances when a preacher should leave his current church rather than be prevented from preaching publicly?

*Chapter Four*

---

# Using the Law

*While [the law] shows…the righteousness alone acceptable to God, it warns, informs, convicts, and lastly condemns, every man of his own unrighteousness. For man, blinded and drunk with self-love, must be compelled to know and to confess his own feebleness and impurity.*
   —John Calvin, *Institutes of the Christian Religion* 2.7.6

Imagine being approached by a surgeon who accosts you out of nowhere and says, "I need to cut you open and remove the cancer inside of you!" You would be frightened and repel such a brash, scalpel-wielding approach. The surgeon never proved you have any kind of condition that requires surgery. His desire to help was met with horror. By failing to expose the underlying problem, the surgeon was not allowed to provide the aid he desired to offer. How much more must an open air preacher expose the reality of indwelling sin in the hearts of his hearers? Only then will they desire the gospel remedy from the Great Physician.

How does an evangelist expose the corruption of sin? It must be done through the skillful exposition and application of God's law.[1]

---

1. Some Reformed Christians do not hold to a strict law/gospel distinction, nor would they claim that the moral law should have a prominent role in evangelism. We respect these men enough to acknowledge that our view of the moral law and evangelism is not universal among Reformed camps, but we do feel, in agreement with the Puritans, that the moral law should have a high place in evangelism, as the rest of this chapter will show.

## The Importance of Using the Law in Open Air Preaching

A preacher should understand the distinction between the moral, civil, and ceremonial law. Only the moral law will play a role in biblical evangelism. The ceremonial laws, which include regulations regarding shellfish, wearing mixed fabrics, or offering regular sacrifices, were abrogated when Jesus said, "It is finished" (John 19:30). The civil laws were also abrogated in their details in New Testament times, since Israel no longer continued to exist as a theocratic nation. But the moral law, summarized in the Ten Commandments, is still enforced by the conscience. The unconverted and even some professing churchgoers resist the preaching of God's moral law, though it is still active within us, as evidenced by our attempt to suppress it when we sin.

God's moral law, under the direction of the Holy Spirit, reveals to men their indwelling depravity. Paul said, "By the law is the knowledge of sin" (Rom. 3:20). Preaching the law plays a vital role in the recovery of Reformed open air evangelism. It exposes the disease of sin and contrasts the holiness of God with mankind's wickedness. The unregenerate are undone because God is holy. They are lost because they have shattered His law and refused to repent and call on the Lord to save them. The purpose of preaching the law is to bring to the natural man a better knowledge of sin. Otherwise the sinner will not turn to Jesus Christ in saving faith. Jesus did not come to save people from bad hair days or foggy wits. He came to save people from their sin—its guilt, corruption, and enslaving power. Only Jesus Christ can save men from their sin, but men must first be made aware of their problem.

The law is given a unique place in God's message. It is the foundation on which the preacher builds the case that the whole Adamic race is under the power and guilt of sin. He must show that man does not obey God. Prior to regeneration we do not love God, nor are we able to (Rom. 3:10–19). This is why the law is to be employed in preaching. The first four commandments refer to how God is to be loved and served. The last six commandments refer to what our behavior should be toward our neighbor. In our fallen condition we do not even love the Lord with all our heart, soul, mind, and strength (Luke 10:27). We do not even love our neighbors as ourselves. Rather, "they are all gone out of the way, they are together become unprofitable; there is none that doeth good, no, not one" (Rom. 3:12). As Calvin states, "The function of the law is that, convicted of our depravity, we may confess our weakness and misery."[2]

**The Law Was Used by Christ and Others in Church History**

How does the preacher prove man's depravity? By unpacking God's commandments and applying them to the hearers. This foundational step in preaching must not be neglected, nor should it be rushed. The preaching of the law shuts men's mouths (Rom. 3:19). It convinces men of the exceeding sinfulness of sin (Rom. 7:13). It alone, under the convicting influence of God's Spirit, will cause men to cry out, "What must I do to be saved?" (Acts 16:30). Our exhortation to men is not "Amend your life" or "Go to church." Our exhortation is repent and "believe on the Lord Jesus Christ, and thou shalt be saved" (Acts 16:31).

Jesus Christ was the greatest evangelist who ever lived. He knew how to expose sin and did not hesitate to do it. With the woman at the well, Jesus exposed her violation of the seventh commandment. With the rich young ruler, He showed his violation of the first and tenth commandments. Rightly could Jesus say about the world, "I testify of it, that the works thereof are evil" (John 7:7). How did He do this? By using the law. Consider His words from the Sermon on the Mount:

> Ye have heard that it was said of them of old time, Thou shalt not kill; and whosoever shall kill shall be in danger of the judgment: but I say unto you, That whosoever is angry with his brother without a cause shall be in danger of the judgment.... Ye have heard that it was said by them of old time, Thou shalt not commit adultery: but I say unto you, That whosoever looketh on a woman to lust after her hath committed adultery with her already in his heart. (Matt. 5:21–22, 27–28)

Jesus used the law in His preaching not only to expose sins of commission (those we take action to commit) but also the sins of omission (those actions we know we should have done but omitted to do). Neglecting a duty or commandment is a sin of omission. Consider the following: "For I was an hungred, and ye gave me no meat: I was thirsty, and ye gave me no drink: I was a stranger, and ye took me not

---

2. Calvin, *Institutes* 4.15.12.

in: naked, and ye clothed me not: sick, and in prison, and ye visited me not" (Matt. 25:42–43). The Lord preached the law to expose sin, which led people to seek the good news or "gospel" about the Shepherd who leads His people into green pastures. Jesus Christ is the Great Physician who came to save the spiritually dead. Jesus is the One who "shall save his people from their sins" (Matt. 1:21), but in doing so they will always realize that they are sinners.

The purpose of preliminary law work (expositing and applying the law) is to humble man, abase him, shut his mouth, and provide the biblical foundation on which conviction of sin is established. In writing to a young friend, John Wesley reportedly counseled him to preach 90 percent law and 10 percent grace. This will be true in many settings, though not all. But in every setting the beauty of the gospel must be contrasted with the false idea of personal good works or self-righteousness. As Iain Murray demonstrates, man must be brought low, not to harm him but to help him look to Jesus: "Preaching [the law] does not regenerate, but in the hand of God it has a key role both in the 'legal conviction,' which is generally preparatory to regeneration, and in setting forth the Savior in whom alone the penitent and the believing find rest."[3] The preacher must magnify how gracious God's salvation is to undeserving, ill-deserving, hell-deserving lawbreakers. The purpose of preaching the law is to exalt the grace of the sovereign God. Dr. Joel Beeke notes how the Puritans practiced the same thing:

> The message of the Bible and the Puritans is: The law has an evangelistic use. Let man try to obey the law for salvation. At first he will think he can do it. Then he will learn that he cannot possibly be as holy as the law demands. Wielded by the Spirit, the law condemns him, pronounces a curse upon him, and declares him liable to the wrath of God and the torments of hell (Gal. 3:10). Finally, he will come to the desperate realization that only God can save him by changing his heart and giving him a new nature. The Spirit brings him to the end of the law, Christ Jesus, as the only righteousness acceptable with God (Gal. 3:24).[4]

---

3. Iain H. Murray, *Revival and Revivalism* (Carlisle, Pa.: Banner of Truth, 1994), 376.
4. Joel Beeke, *Puritan Evangelism* (Grand Rapids: Reformation Heritage Books, 2007), 41–42.

Dr. Martyn Lloyd-Jones notes the same thing when commenting on law and gospel preaching in the past: "Great evangelical preachers three hundred years ago in the time of the Puritans, and two hundred years ago in the time of Whitefield and others, always engaged in what they called a preliminary 'law work.'"[5]

## How the Open Air Preacher Should Use the Law

So how does the preacher apply the law skillfully? Again, we look to Jesus, whose primary method for applying the law was through questions. In the parable of the good Samaritan, He asks, "Which now of these three, thinkest thou, was neighbour unto him that fell among the thieves?" (Luke 10:36). He asks a lawyer, "What is written in the law? how readest thou?" (Luke 10:26). In a similar way, a preacher should not hesitate to ask unbelievers, How many times have you lied? How many times have you stolen something? Have you ever looked at someone with lust? How many times? Although strict formulas should be avoided, questions like these help the preacher to get sin out into the open. Most people in our culture think they are good or righteous. This approach exposes the folly of such a view.[6]

But deeper application must then be made. Why have you committed these sins? Why is sin so vile? Why must you repent and believe? What does it mean to repent? The hearers must be shown that they are fallen children of Adam. They have sinned against God, the pure and holy Creator of the universe. They must be shown that God is provoked. He does not owe men salvation. He is the potter who has the right to form vessels for honor or dishonor (Rom. 9:21). The preacher must impress on his hearers that they must repent of their sin and turn in faith to Jesus, the "name which is above every name" (Phil. 2:9). He must emphasize that the Holy Spirit alone can regenerate an evil, sin-loving heart into one that desires and lives for God. His hearers must be told to

---

5. D. M. Lloyd-Jones, *Romans, Exposition of Chapters 7.1–8.4* (Carlisle, Pa.: Banner of Truth, 1973), 114.

6. Credit must here be given to Ray Comfort, who has been shown much grace to understand and apply the preliminary work of law preaching. He has been instrumental in aiding an almost ubiquitous rediscovery of this foundation of biblical evangelism as well as proving that preachers do not need to dig a new well, since the old well still supplies living water.

call on Jesus Christ to deliver them from the wrath to come, since "whosoever shall call upon the name of the Lord shall be saved" (Rom. 10:13).

We recall a time at the University of Massachusetts–Boston when a team of open air preachers was receiving a high level of abuse. Students were trying to push them off the wall where they were preaching. The campus police were doing nothing to protect them. One student, covered in tattoos, came within inches of the preachers' faces, screaming profanities and insisting they get off his campus. One of the preachers went over and asked the heckler what his problem was. While the student continued to pour forth abuse, the preacher noticed he had two Hebrew letters tattooed on his neck. He asked him if he was Jewish. The student said he was and that the letters spelled his name, Ezra. The preacher asked, "Do you realize you were named after the man who did precisely what we have been doing? Ezra elevated himself above the people and preached in the open air. Do you believe Moses was a Hebrew who received the law on Mount Sinai?" Ezra said he did. The preacher asked him, "Have you kept God's law?"

The preacher continued to use the law with the student. The more the preacher asked questions about Ezra's obedience to God's law, the more nervous Ezra appeared. Eventually he turned red, shut his mouth, and asked if there was any hope for him. Only then did the gospel of Jesus Christ make sense! Only then did the person and work of Christ become lovely to him! Ezra's eyes filled with tears. He began to apologize profusely. The Holy Spirit used the law to stop Ezra's mouth and give him an awareness of "sin, and of righteousness, and of judgment" (John 16:8). Christ looked wonderfully desirable to Ezra. The preacher told him to repent of his sin and call on the name of the Lord so that he might be saved. Before Ezra left, he gratefully accepted a New Testament Bible. This is why the open air preacher must trust in the converting influence of God's law as foundational for the evangelistic message.

## Different Uses of the Moral Law

Calvin taught that the moral law has three uses. It is critical for the preacher to bear these distinctions in mind. The first use of the law is similar to a mirror, showing us the depravity of our hearts when compared to God's righteousness. R. C. Sproul summarizes the first use in this way: "On the one hand, the law of God reflects and mirrors the perfect righteousness of God. The law tells us much about who God is. Perhaps more important, the law illustrates human sinfulness.... Here the law acts as a severe schoolmaster who drives us to Christ."[7]

The second use of the law, according to Calvin, is to restrain evil: "The law, in and of itself, cannot change human hearts. It can, however, serve to protect the righteous from the unjust."[8] In other words, the law is useful in civil and secular matters, enforcing penalties in this life.

The third use of the law is to reveal the will of God to the conscience of believers. The law acts like a governor or enforcer for those who love Christ. Consider Sproul's comments on the matter: "As born-again children of God, the law enlightens us as to what is pleasing to our Father, whom we seek to serve. The Christian delights in the law of God as God Himself delights in it."[9] Jesus Himself said, "If you love me, keep my commandments" (John 14:15). This third use of God's law acts as a referee who blows the whistle whenever we step out of bounds. It does not justify us as Christians, but it does alert us whenever we deviate from our duty to love God and love our neighbor as ourselves.

The skillful open air preacher will primarily emphasize the first use of the law. The second use could be seen by the unregenerate as a kind of work that men can do in their own strength, and it will likely distract from the free offer of forgiveness of sins and imputed righteousness. The third use of the law is helpful in the work of progressive sanctification and should be primarily employed in the local church or wherever believers are gathered.

It is important to remember that open air preaching should not end with the law. When preaching, usually a minority will seem to be under the influence of the Holy Spirit. Although the law should be used as preliminary work, above all else people must hear of Christ's person, work, and resurrection, followed by the call to repent and believe. Speaking about the law and judgment without reference to Christ's atonement and resurrection would be in vain.

---

7. R. C. Sproul, *Essential Truths of the Christian Faith* (Carol Stream, Ill.: Tyndale House, 1992), 257.
8. Calvin, *Institutes* 2.1.3–7.
9. Sproul, *Essential Truths*, 257.

Whether God converts, convicts, or condemns is up to His own sovereign will. We are called to be preachers of the good news, but that good news must be properly framed by a solid foundation of law preaching. Spurious conversions are often a direct result of preachers not magnifying the holiness of God and His law. God has acted from love to solve the problem of sin, without negotiating His justice. Jesus Christ bore on the cross the punishment His people deserved, and His righteousness, displayed through a life of obedience to God on earth, is now imputed to us as believers: "Not by works of righteousness which we have done, but according to his mercy he saved us, by the washing of regeneration, and renewing of the Holy Ghost" (Titus 3:5). This message must not be overlooked.

Today, the gospel is often proclaimed in a man-centered and God-dishonoring way. By exposing sin and man's inability to please God, however, the hearer is rightly abased. He is shown the darkness of his spiritual state and that God alone can save him. Many churchgoers today have been reared in Arminianism, most of them without knowing it. A presupposed notion of libertarian free will exists in most churches today, so most Christians believe that mankind has an innate ability to make a decision for Christ. The law removes all confidence in man's ability: he is left naked, undone, and desperate when contrasted with the required perfection of the law. Preaching the law plows the soil of man's heart, which is then ready for the gospel seed to be sown: "Him that cometh to me I will in no wise cast out" (John 6:37).

It is important to remember that all Christians remain simultaneously justified and a sinner (*simul justus et peccator*). Luther reminds us by this Latin phrase that the most sanctified preacher still sins and falls short of perfect obedience to God. The skill in applying the law is to contrast the hearers with God's nature, and specifically Jesus Christ, not the preacher. God's grace must ever be before our own eyes as well (1 Cor. 15:10). The preacher struggles and wars against indwelling sin, so the law instructs both preacher and hearer to constantly look to Christ. Paul said, "Not as though I had already attained, either were already perfect: but I follow after, if that I may apprehend that for which also I am apprehended of Christ Jesus" (Phil. 3:12). Let it be so with the open air preacher as well.

## Questions

1. What are some ways to apply the law while preaching?

2. In what situations should the open air preacher not apply the law?

3. Do you agree that you will not properly exalt the glory of the gospel unless you preach the law? Why or why not?

# Chapter Five

# Using Apologetics

*I hold that unless you believe in God you can logically believe in nothing else.*
          —Cornelius Van Til, *Why I Believe in God*

Occasionally apologetics—defending the faith (1 Peter 3:15) or "contend[ing] for the faith" (Jude 3)—will be required in open air preaching. Every preacher should make a serious, self-conscious effort to become better prepared to "give an answer to every man that asketh you a reason of the hope that is in you" in a way that presents Christ as set apart or sanctified as "Lord God in your hearts" (1 Peter 3:15). Here too a biblical approach is critical. There are many schools or methods of apologetics these days. In this chapter we will argue for a presuppositional approach to defending the faith when preaching in public. This approach is a distinctively Reformed apologetic that begins and ends with the God of the Scriptures.[1]

## Presuppositional Apologetics Defined and the Impossibility of Neutrality

Unbelievers pose many questions and criticisms to the preacher regarding Christianity. As Greg Bahnsen notes, "The resistance may

---

1. We owe much of this chapter to Cornelius Van Til, Greg Bahnsen, and Gordon Clark. We consider these men to be leading presuppositional apologists, although the tradition began much earlier with John Calvin, Augustine, and most importantly with the authors of Scripture.

be emotional (ridicule, disdain, apathy) or behavioral (living disobe-
diently, refusing to give thanks or offer worship), but sometimes it is
intellectual."[2] The preacher should endeavor to answer each of these
challenges in a way that points to the gospel. Just as importantly, his
answer must be consistent with the convictions of Reformed theology.
He must never assume that neutral ground exists between a believer
and an unbeliever nor that the unbeliever is unbiased or open-minded,
especially in light of biblical revelation: "Unbelievers are not neutral,
since they are by nature children of wrath (Eph. 2:3), are hostile to God
(Eph. 4:17–18), and suffer from the noetic effects of sin (Rom. 7:23;
Luke 24:24)."[3]

This is the problem with evidential and classical approaches to
apologetics. The Christian presents evidence for the existence of God
or some other Christian truth claim to the unbeliever, who then sits in
the place of a judge, evaluating the evidence. God's existence is on trial.
Maybe it is the historical reliability of Jesus or the resurrection or the
virgin birth. The unbeliever goes on to determine that the evidence is
lacking. Or, granting that the evidence is persuasive, the unbeliever goes
on to say he still needs more evidence. If nothing else, the unbeliever
will go home and do research to justify himself against the argument
just put forward by the preacher, which means the preacher must then
arm himself with further arguments to combat this new evidence. This
cycle will then be repeated over and over. But unbelievers are biased
against God and will always attempt to act in accordance with the "van-
ity of their mind" (Eph. 4:17), whose thoughts are always hostile to God
(Col. 1:21). What the unbeliever needs is a new mind, not new evidence.
He needs the new birth, not new arguments about God.

Remember that the open air preacher is dealing with unbelievers
whose worldview assumes that the human mind has ultimate authority.
The unbeliever will make himself the reference point for interpreting
reality and will subordinate God's Word to his own autonomous[4] rea-

---

2. Greg Bahnsen, *Van Til's Apologetic* (Phillipsburg, N.J.: P&R Publishing, 1998),
699–700.

3. Sonny Hernandez, *Apologetics Primer for the Armed Forces* (Clarksville, Tenn.:
Reforming America Ministries, 2017), 8.

4. Autonomy means "self-rule" or "self-law."

soning, which is at war with God. The preacher, to be consistent with his biblical worldview, must show that all facts reveal the existence of God and His plan as found in Scripture. Or, to put it another way, reality is what God says it is in Scripture. All human knowledge must be subordinated to that plan. This is why no neutral ground exists between the believer and the unbeliever. All ground belongs to Christ. The natural man must always borrow from Christ's universe even to deny His existence.

The preacher must labor to show that the unbeliever's worldview will always be untenable or inconsistent. He must then turn the tables by pointing out that, by contrast, Christianity is the only worldview that is consistent with what it claims. The unbeliever must be shown that his worldview cannot make sense of reality without borrowing from Christian presuppositions. For instance, logic, science, mathematics, morality, and other disciplines cannot be valid unless grounded on the objective, eternal, unchangeable God of the Bible. Likewise, any interpretation of reality must be thoroughly Christian if it is to be accurate or consistent, since Christ has made all things and is the only way man's redemption is possible. For an unbeliever to say he can know anything at all is impossible unless the triune God of the Bible is the reason for it. Truth is that which conforms to the mind of God as known through Christ (Col. 2:3; John 1:9).

### Unbelievers Always Aim at Preserving Their Autonomy

Professing atheists and agnostics deny the need for any form of divine authority. Unbelievers worship the supposed autonomy of human reason, which is their attempt to suppress the truth of God. This is why any concept of authority that stands above human reason is unacceptable to unbelievers.

But the Bible teaches no such thing as an actual atheist or agnostic. Consider Romans 1, for instance. Paul, in the original Greek text, describes the unbelieving man as knowing *the* God (v. 21), which implies an intellectual awareness of God. The definite article proves it is not a vague or abstract awareness of some God or deity but the very God of the universe. Most Christian apologists attempt to argue for some version of God or deity. They assume that if they can get the unbeliever to admit of the existence of a God, then gradually they will come to believe in *the* God. But a god is different than the true God, so this approach is dishonest. The Bible shows that the unbeliever already has knowledge of God, which is why Paul can say "because" (v. 21) men have this knowledge, they are "without excuse," or literally "without an apologetic" or "defense" for their unrighteous and reprobate living (vv. 20, 23–31). Their thanklessness (v. 21) and foolish thinking (vv. 21–22) are not done in ignorance. God's wrath justly rests on all men outside of Christ because He has manifested Himself to them in such a way that they know "that which may be known of God" (v. 19). Whether someone lives in the jungles of South America or in urbanized China, they clearly see God's divine attributes (v. 20). Every human without exception knows "the truth of God" (v. 25). But unbelievers do not deem it worthwhile to "retain God in their knowledge" (v. 28), choosing rather to suppress the truth by means of their unrighteousness (v. 18). Paul is claiming that the unbeliever has definite beliefs about God and possesses full and overwhelming "proof" for those beliefs. This is why there is no such thing as a genuine atheist or agnostic and why it is nearly always a wasted effort to give evidence for God's existence rather than call for the unbeliever to repent of his supposed autonomy and submit to the evidence he already has.[5] This can be done by pointing out the inconsistency of so-called autonomous reasoning.

One year we witnessed this firsthand while engaging a college student from UTEP who said he was an atheist. We told him he was not an atheist, showing him from the Scriptures that he was merely suppressing the truth about God. The student persisted all semester, but we continued confronting him with Scripture, showing him the inconsistency of his professed worldview. After fifteen weeks the student came up and said he needed to confess something: he was not really an atheist. He admitted that no one is an atheist. He did not need evidence—he needed to be confronted with the Word of God. Within six months the student began attending an evangelical church.

The unbeliever's problem or lack of belief is his heart, not evidence. His problem is his hatred for God. He hates the existence of God and His written revelation. He hates the idea that God is King of

---

5. Greg Bahnsen influences much of the language here.

the universe. The unbeliever is actively at war against God, whether or not he admits it. Since the time the unbeliever came "from the womb" (Ps. 58:3), he has been living in rebellion, so naturally he has an axe to grind against God.

Denying God's existence or other truth claims of Scripture is a defense mechanism to quiet the conscience. It is an attempt to sin boldly without any regard for the Judge of the universe. But he does regard this Judge: the unbeliever knows that every square inch of the universe testifies to His reality. This is why the unbeliever does everything in his power to suppress such truth and why he needs a new heart, not more evidence. He needs to submit to the evidence he already has, and only the power of God working through the preached gospel can do that. Consider Van Til's remarks: "Men ought, says Calvin following Paul, to believe in God, for each one is surrounded with a superabundance of evidence with respect to him. The whole universe is lit up by God. Scripture requires men to accept its interpretation of history as true without doubt. Doubt of this kind...is as unreasonable as a child asking whether he has parents and, after looking at the evidence, concluding that he probably has."[6]

All people have a personal worldview or commitment that acts as chief authority in their life. This is what the open air preacher must drive home and expose. An unbeliever's authority will be himself, and it will always prove inconsistent. Ever since Adam ate the forbidden fruit, men have tried to make themselves God. Naturally hostile in mind toward God (1 Cor. 1:21), they consider themselves to be the ultimate criterion of truth and set themselves up as knowing the universe better than God. They reference everything in light of their own reason or desire, which of course is limited and prone to mistakes. Adam and Eve did the same thing when they bit into the fruit, but without God as a reference, how can the unbeliever be certain his reason is even valid? How can he assume to know anything at all? Surely the unbeliever will admit he does not have exhaustive knowledge of the universe and that he is prone to make mistakes. This is the folly of making one's self the standard of truth.

---

6. Cornelius Van Til, *The Reformed Pastor and Modern Thought* (Nutley, N.J.: Presbyterian and Reformed, 1971), 32–34.

## The Only Hope for Meaning and Rationality Is Christ

The rational man, the moral man, and the scientific man all operate on the assumption that the ultimate reference point is the human being. As Bahnsen notes, the open air preacher must show that the ultimate source of truth in any field is found in Christ alone: "The fact of science and its progress is inexplicable except upon the presupposition that the world is made and controlled by God through Christ and that man is made and renewed in the image of God through Christ."[7] It is impossible for the unbeliever to account for science, logic, morality, uniformity in the universe, or any other law or fact apart from Christ. Biblical apologetics demonstrates to the unbeliever the irrationality and even impossibility of all other worldviews other than historic Christianity: "The way to prove the truth of Christianity, then, is to take the conflicting worldviews of the Christian and the non-Christian—with their opposing presuppositions and theories of knowledge, in terms of which particular claims are disputed back and forth—and press for a critical internal analysis of each one, looking for philosophical inconsistency and absurdity. This is the way to refute the unbeliever's bedrock presuppositions, showing the intellectual impossibility of any worldview that is contrary to Christianity."[8]

Meaning can be accounted for only by God's Word, apart from which the capacity to reason would be impossible. God is the reason for objective, unchangeable laws in the universe, such as logic or truth. God's knowledge of the universe is exhaustive because He is the creator and sustainer of it. Thus, God must be the chief authority for everything we do because everything begins with and continues through Him. And more specifically, the written revelation of this God must be the source by which everything else is to be evaluated.

The unbeliever always uses his God-given reasoning capacity to make any claim concerning that same God, even if it is to deny His existence. Without an acknowledgment of God, the unbeliever is forced to say he knows his reasoning is valid because his reasoning makes it so. But his reasoning powers are subject to mistakes. They are far from omniscient. The Christian knows his reasoning is valid because it

---

7. Bahnsen, *Van Til's Apologetic*, 710.
8. Bahnsen, *Van Til's Apologetic*, 701.

conforms to an objective, unchangeable source—the triune God—and His written revelation, the Scriptures.

Without belief in the God of Scripture, it is impossible for the unbeliever to prove anything at all, not only in religion but also in logic, science, experience, history, or morality: "This is what is meant by the 'presuppositional method' of defending the faith. It calls upon the unbeliever to confess his intellectual rebellion and ruin, and then to submit in faith, thanksgiving, and obedience to the claims of the self-attesting Christ."[9]

**Man Is Always in Need of God's Special Revelation**

The Scriptures must be the ultimate criterion of truth for every open air preacher, and no less so when doing apologetics. Many ministers claim that the Bible is the ultimate criterion for truth but then compromise when defending or contending for the faith. They will take a more "neutral" position when it comes to revelation. As Bahnsen notes, a preacher must stand on the authority of the Bible in every aspect of his life, which includes dealing with unbelievers: "Since sin has come into the world, God's interpretation of the facts must come in finished, written form and be comprehensive in character. God continues to reveal himself in the facts of the created world, but the sinner needs to interpret every one of them in the clearer light of Scripture. Every thought on every subject must become obedient to the requirement of God as he speaks in his Word; every thought must be brought into subjection to Christ."[10]

Ever since God spoke to Adam in paradise before the fall, He has used supernatural communication to deal with His people.[11] This is the case even though sinners, apart from the Holy Spirit, will always attempt to eradicate God's Word. Biblical apologetics does not ask the unbeliever to consider the possibility of the Bible's authority. This again is the difference between biblical apologetics and more traditional or evidential approaches. It begins with the Bible as self-authoritative and

9. Bahnsen, *Van Til's Apologetic*, 701.
10. Bahnsen, *Van Til's Apologetic*, 70–71.
11. "The Bible is the supernatural communication of God to creatures who have become sinners." Bahnsen, *Van Til's Apologetic*, 713.

self-attesting, and it claims that without such revelation, no meaningful interpretation of anything could be possible. Christ as God speaks
in the Bible with absolute authority. Thus, the Bible does not appeal to
human reason for its justification, otherwise humans would be posi-
tioned as more authoritative than God's Word. Rather, the Bible comes
to the human being with absolute authority and demands that men
submit to it.

Some criticize the presuppositional approach as being viciously
circular since it begins with the Bible as self-authoritative and self-
attesting. These critics fail to understand that every argument about
chief authorities must in some sense be "circular." If you are arguing
with an unbeliever about the existence of God or the truth claims of
Christianity, he will tell you they are wrong because he says they are
wrong. The unbeliever may appeal to something outside of himself to
make that claim, but he will be the one who judges the evidence to
be more authoritative than the Bible. In other words, he begins with
himself as the ultimate authority and assumes it is self-attesting. When
pressed, he will be forced to admit that the "evidence" about God's existence or other truth claims found in Scripture is judged to be lacking,
just because he says so. His argument circles around himself. Even if he
brings in the writings or evidence from some historian or scientist to
validate his point, he still must make the judgment that the historian
or scientist is more reliable than the Bible. Thus, his own reason will
always be the reference point. But the open air preacher must never
give up the Bible as the ultimate reference point. Anything that contradicts the Bible is wrong because the Bible, as God's revelation, is always
the ultimate authority, not man. The Bible as God's revelation is suffi-
cient and inerrant since it comes from an eternal, infallible Being who
created and sustains the universe.

Van Til deals with this charge of circular reasoning in several of his
works: "Now if it be called circular reasoning when we hold it necessary
to presuppose the existence of God, we are not ashamed of it because
we are firmly convinced that all forms of reasoning that leave God out
of account will end in ruin."[12] Or consider again his remarks on the
inspiration of Scripture: "The only alternative to 'circular reasoning' as

---

12. Van Til, as quoted in Bahnsen, *Van Til's Apologetic*, 519.

engaged in by Christians, no matter on what point they speak, is that of reasoning on the basis of isolated facts and isolated minds, with the result that there is no possibility of reasoning at all. Unless as sinners we have an absolutely inspired Bible, we have no absolute God interpreting reality for us, and unless we have an absolute God interpreting reality for us, there is no true interpretation at all."[13]

Also note that circular reasoning is different from a circular argument or vicious circular reasoning, which are fallacies. Van Til notes that circular reasoning is perfectly valid: "The only alternative to starting with the 'I AM' of Christ is to start with the 'I am' of man in some such way.... Thus false circular reasoning stands over against true circular reasoning."[14] Starting with the Bible as self-authoritative and self-attesting is in no way some kind of lesser or invalid form of presentation. Everyone uses an ultimate authority for making a case. Presuppositional apologetics rightly posits that the only options on the table are God's revelation or man's reason. But only God's revelation can be held as authoritative without inconsistency or error.

### Cults and World Religions

Presuppositional apologetics can be used to challenge other religious faiths as well. The approach would be no different from confronting atheism. The open air preacher must internally examine whatever worldview is being presented from the viewpoint of that religion. By doing so, it will become evident that contradictions exist on either an epistemological or metaphysical level, as in non-Christian religions. Religions that stem from or have been influenced by the Bible, such as Islam, Mormonism, or Jehovah's Witnesses, can be treated as Christian heresies and reasoned against by using Scripture itself to show where they have departed from the truth.

Although it is helpful to have an understanding of other religions and cults when defending or contending for the faith, it is just as useful to have a grasp of biblical doctrine and church history. Being able

---

13. Cornelius Van Til, *An Introduction to Systematic Theology* (Nutley, N.J.: Presbyterian and Reformed, 1974), 43.

14. Cornelius Van Til, *Christianity in Conflict* (Philadelphia: Westminster Theological Seminary, 1962–1964 (syllabus), chap. 9.

to clearly articulate orthodox doctrine or certain contexts of church history will be useful against most world religions or cults, which are usually by-products if not duplications of prior heretical movements.[15] Knowledge of church history will help the open air preacher identify such heresies and know how the Christians of old defended the faith against them. This is why the preacher would best spend his time studying doctrine and church history rather than evidential arguments for the existence of God or other Christian truth claims. He would also benefit from studying the specific religions or cults he is likely to engage, which includes Darwinian evolution (which is closer to a faith-based religion than science) for those preaching in the West.

The preacher must also be sensitive to sincere questions, as opposed to those intended to stump him. Like Satan, the unbeliever will often twist the Scriptures in an attempt to make the preacher contradict himself. Spending time with such persons could be an example of casting "pearls before swine" (Matt. 7:6). In such cases a preacher should avoid being entangled in arguments and stick to the preaching of the cross. However, when encountering someone who is sincerely wrestling or having difficulty with some doctrine of the faith, such as the resurrection or the virgin birth, using Scripture instead of classical or evidential approaches is advised. As Greg Bahnsen explains,

> Traditional evidentialism does not handle the evidence as it should. It pretends that there are neutral facts or neutral methods for examining the facts.... In every presentation of a factual argument for Christianity, the defender of the faith is implicitly— if not explicitly—challenging the unbeliever with an entire system or Christian worldview of which the fact is a part. "Facts" do not stand outside of systems of thought, as though they could help us to choose among them. In any factual argument, whether attention is drawn to it or not, two worldviews are set next to each other for comparison.[16]

---

15. This includes Islam and even Marxism, both of which are spin-offs in many ways of orthodox Christianity.

16. Bahnsen, *Van Til's Apologetic*, 641.

The open air preacher must constantly be seeking wisdom from the Holy Spirit. Each apologetic encounter will be different, but the aim must be the command to repent and believe in the Lord Jesus. The goal is not necessarily to prove God or the Bible, nor should it be to win an argument. The preacher must be about showing that all men are without excuse for their unbelief. At the end of the day, only the Holy Spirit can give faith to the unbeliever, but we are called on to present God's truth in a biblical, Christ-centered way. This is why the presuppositional approach to defending the faith is best. Even R. C. Sproul, an opponent of presuppositional apologetics, admits "the existence of God is the supreme *proto*-supposition for all theoretical thought. God's existence is the chief element in constructing any worldview. To deny this chief premise is to set one's sails for the island of nihilism. This is the darkest continent of the darkened mind—the ultimate paradise of the fool."[17] This is what a preacher must be eager to expose and why he must make a concerted effort to better contend for and defend the faith in a biblical, God-honoring manner, and in such a way that is precise (Acts 18:26).

---

17. R. C. Sproul, *The Consequences of Ideas: Understanding the Concepts That Shaped Our World* (Wheaton, Ill.: Crossway, 2000), 171.

## Questions

1. What is the relationship between apologetics and the gospel?

2. Can the gospel be preached without using apologetics?

3. Why must the open air preacher refuse to give up his presupposition that the Bible is his ultimate authority?

# PART TWO

# THE TASK OF OPEN AIR PREACHING

# Chapter Six

# The Preacher's Character

*A man entered the chapel, having "his pockets filled with stones, in order to do injury to the preacher; but when he saw the tears running down his cheeks, and witnessed the bowels of compassion he evinced for poor dying sinners... down went the stones."*
—Mr. Sherman on the power of Whitefield's tenderness (*The Christian Witness and Church Members' Magazine*, 1857)

How does the open air preacher get past the fact that he stumbles "in many things" (James 3:2), unlike the King he proclaims? He must watch his heart with all diligence, always abiding in Christ, who was so closely identified with God the Father that He could make the amazing statement, "He that hath seen me hath seen the Father" (John 14:9). But what about His servants, the preachers? Sadly, none of us can say, "If you've seen me, the preacher, you've seen Jesus." Without love for God and for others, we are merely a "tinkling cymbal" (1 Cor. 13:1), and every departure from loving God and our neighbor is sin. So how does an imperfect preacher, who is in the process of being sanctified, dare open his mouth about the sinless Redeemer?

## Consecration to Christ Is Necessary

"The just [those whom God declares righteous through faith in Jesus Christ] shall live by faith" is a simple statement with profound consequences (Heb. 10:38). The open air preacher must have a faith that looks to Jesus with utter consecration. He must have a heart devoted to God and the advancement of His glory, no matter the cost. Therefore, this issue of consecration, or of keeping the heart set apart for the things of God, must begin and end by looking unto Jesus, "the author and finisher of our faith" (Heb. 12:2). It is not enough to throw up our hands and excuse ourselves for the constant imperfections in our life. The preacher must abide in Christ, always hungering for more holiness.

Consider the following example from Jesus, who cried to God, "not as I will, but as thou wilt" (Matt. 26:39). In the garden of Gethsemane, Jesus was willing to deny His own will for the sake of doing "the will of him that sent me" (John 6:38). The first aspect of consecration in the life of a preacher must be a determination to do the will of God. It is one thing to write such a command, but establishing practical guidelines for carrying it out is an entirely different and more difficult task. In fact, considering our own proclivity to sin, nothing short of God, who "worketh in you both to will and to do" (Phil. 2:13) will suffice. Therefore, separation unto God is critical. This is what it means to be holy or sanctified. A constant examination of the motions and motives of one's heart is necessary for every person who dares to preach. Where has my heart been today? What have I held affection for? What motivated me to do such and such a thing? These questions must constantly be asked, for "if ye live after the flesh, ye shall die: but if ye through the Spirit do mortify the deeds of the body, ye shall live" (Rom. 8:13). The preacher must constantly be about the business of crucifying the flesh in order to better carry out the deeds of the Spirit. But how does he go about this?

## Consecration Requires Separation from Sin, Self, and the World

To be consecrated to God involves three primary aspects. First, it requires a separation from sin: "Let every one that nameth the name of Christ depart from iniquity" (2 Tim. 2:19). Historic Christianity teaches about sins of commission and sins of omission. Consider first a few specific sins that an open air preacher will be tempted to commit. We tend to be men of action. We are prone to be brash and unloving at times. Preachers in general are usually exposed to the temptation of promoting one's self, whether through preaching or social media. Even the most sanctified preacher must be on constant guard not to show-boat or make the message or his ministry about himself. We have been given letters from the King, and our job is to preach them, not elevate ourselves. We must preach for Christ's glory, not our own. Self must die! An advantage of open air preaching is the opportunity for practicing self-denial. Whether venting one's anger and frustration against the lost or having a holier-than-thou attitude, it is sin. The wrath of man does not produce the righteousness of God (James 1:20). Consider the hecklers who come against the open air preacher. We are in sin any time we lash out against them in anger, respond with a belittling comeback, or put them down in a clever way. These are examples of a lack of consecration to Christ, yet how many times do we act this way? This is why it is crucial for the preacher to constantly analyze himself to see what needs to be mortified.

As a disciple of Christ, the preacher is called to "deny himself, and take up his cross daily" (Luke 9:23). Any notion of self-pity, self-exaltation, or self-righteousness must be crucified. Our corrupt nature must be turned over to death as we walk in consecration to Jesus. The same is true when we are preaching. Open air preaching is more fluid and lively than pulpit preaching. The dynamics will always leave the preacher exposed to reactions from his hearers. Defensiveness or having to get the last word in with the heckler is a sign that self is very much alive. We must be fools for Christ. It matters not if people think we look foolish. We preach Christ, not ourselves. We are not called to please ourselves, but our Master (Rom. 15:1). As God grows us in sanctification, these layers of self-love must continually be mortified.

The open air preacher must also be separated from the world. Any carnality or love for the world will cause him to be unstable in all his ways (James 1:8). He must be trained to aim his gospel cannon against the world and the culture, which is why we are told to "marvel not, my brethren, if the world hate you" (1 John 3:13). Our Lord reminds us, "It hated me before it hated you" (John 15:18). The preacher must not expect to be loved, accepted, or praised by the world. Unfortunately, many churchgoers assume that if the world hates you, especially when evangelizing, then you are doing something wrong. But the Scriptures tell us "all that will live godly in Christ Jesus shall suffer persecution"

(2 Tim. 3:12). The preacher should avoid all reliance on worldly wisdom since "the world by wisdom knew not God" (1 Cor. 1:21). He must be prepared to be the offscouring of the world, which will be a rude awakening for the man who is not ready for it. As he preaches, he will discover that he is an aroma of death because the world does not love Christ but rather its own (John 15:19).

### What about the "Sinless Perfection" Doctrine?

It seems appropriate at this point to address the problem of "sinless perfection" preachers. They have been a bane to the Reformed evangelism community for many decades. These are usually the "shock and awe" preachers. They operate from a Pelagian perspective that denies original sin along with the ongoing reality of our own fallenness and indwelling sin.[1] This type of preacher will tell the crowd he has not sinned in ten years. Some would say thirty years. Of course this attitude is abysmal since it blatantly contradicts the Scriptures: "If we say that we have no sin, we deceive ourselves, and the truth is not in us" (1 John 1:8). It is difficult to believe that such preachers have ever been born again, much less lived a sinless life. To exist in such a depth of spiritual darkness indicates an unregenerate soul. These preachers haunt college campuses and other places of gathering. They abuse people with their "shock and awe" approach, using extreme language to get a crowd before promoting their unbiblical doctrine.

Spiritual perfection does not exist this side of the grave. The Christian will move in a sinless direction, meaning growth in grace and mortification of sin. But the Bible nowhere teaches this chimera of sinless perfection. Christ's righteousness is gloriously imputed to us, but there is never an impartation of righteousness, which is different. Preachers must acknowledge our experiential imperfection and cling by faith to Christ, not our own righteousness. Christ sanctifies His people. Our works do not keep us saved, Christ does. Like the apostle Paul, we need to be preachers who admit "not as though I had already

---

1. Pelagius lived in the late fourth century AD. He taught that God would not require a man to do that which he could not perform. Hence Pelagius denied original sin and the vitiating effects of the fall.

attained, either were already perfect," but rather, we long for the day when we can cast off sin forever (Phil. 3:12).[2]

How does the preacher deal with the fact that on the one hand we must be holy and righteous in truth, and on the other hand our heart is still divided in its affections? Hopefully our sins are more often those of omission rather than commission. Nevertheless, the preacher must be quick to confess sin and forsake it. Martin Luther was right to point out that we need to live a life of continual repentance, looking more and more to Jesus, who "save[s] his people from their sins" (Matt. 1:21).[3] As preachers, we of all people should be able to articulate in truth how God has been powerfully preserving and freeing us from our fallenness. If a preacher is unable to testify to such sanctification, he should tarry a while longer before plunging into ministry. Our devotion to Christ is more important than our devotion to the ministry. Preachers should have a demonstrable level of experiential sanctification in their lives, though they will still be far short of perfection.

## The Need for Humility

Jesus was the paragon of humility, condescending to take on human flesh and exercise obedience to the Father in all things. Considering all the great biblical truths of Reformed doctrine, one might think humility would come easily to Reformed preachers. Yet it is surprisingly rare. How quickly we can be provoked by the unbelievers to whom we preach. Even sadder is how quickly we are provoked by our brethren. Jesus said, "Without me ye can do nothing" (John 15:5), which is especially true regarding humility. Without God's presence, preachers are powerless to advance His kingdom. This includes humility. Unless God anoints the preached Word with the power of the Holy Spirit, nothing will happen.[4]

---

2. John Owen's *Sin and Temptation in the Life of the Believer* and Sinclair Ferguson's *Devotion to God* are two helpful books the open air preacher would do well to read regularly.

3. "When our Lord and Master Jesus Christ said 'Repent,' he intended that the entire life of believers should be repentance." Stephen J. Nichols, ed., *Martin Luther's Ninety-Five Theses* (Phillipsburg, N.J.: P&R Publishing, 2002), 23.

4. All Christians (especially Reformed preachers) should annually read Andrew Murray's *Humility*. It is a classic on this aspect of Christlikeness.

One year we led a team of preachers into an abandoned graveyard. Once in front of the graves, we asked each of these experienced preachers to preach for ten minutes. The purpose was to show that dry bones do not come back to life. It would require a miracle. Every open air preacher should go to a graveyard and preach his best sermon as loud as he is able, calling for the dead bones to come to life. This will show how little control one has over the spiritually dead. This should produce humility. We are powerless unless God acts. Jesus said that after we have done all that is commanded of us, we are to return and admit we are "unprofitable servants" (Luke 17:10).

Deep awareness of our own unworthiness and helplessness will be fertile soil for growing humility. We must decrease, that He might increase: "Why look ye so earnestly on us, as though by our own power or holiness we had made this man to walk?" (Acts 3:12). Let a preacher be constantly aware of his spiritual poverty before God and, by His grace, he will become useful to the Master. Humble yourself and God will lift you up.

**The Necessity of Spiritual Disciplines**
The open air preacher must devote himself to spiritual disciplines, in particular prayer, Bible study, and fasting. Jesus had a serious life of prayer, devoting entire nights to it on some occasions. Preachers know we should be devoted to prayer, but are we? I have never met a preacher who says he prays too much. I have never met a preacher who says he prays enough. If the Lord of glory spent long sessions in prayer, so must we: "They that wait upon the LORD shall renew their strength; they shall mount up with wings as eagles; they shall run, and not be weary; and they shall walk, and not faint" (Isa. 40:31). Prayer is a privilege. It gives us access to God and is the secret activity through which the preacher is strengthened. We must set aside time for regular prayer. The preacher must schedule private prayer as the highest priority of his day. It cannot be left until we feel like praying, because it will likely never happen. Prayer is hard work. It must be both scheduled and spontaneous. If a preacher is too busy to pray, then he is too busy! Some evangelists make it a priority to pray at least as much as they preach. Tarrying before God's face in humble dependence is certainly the secret to having power with

God and men. Our Father loves to strengthen His people when they seek Him in prayer. Power belongs to God, and we must believe that He who sees in secret will reward us openly (Matt. 6:6).

It also goes without saying that the preacher must be a student of God's Word. He must be a theologian who seeks to know the God of the Word rather than merely the Word of God. The Lord has exalted His Word even above His name (Ps. 138:2). Since the preacher is unpacking a message from God and applying it to his hearers, he must be a man who hides God's Word in his heart. He must see it as daily bread for his own soul before he preaches it to others. He must let the Word of God dwell in him richly, finding Christ everywhere in Scripture: "I am the living bread," Jesus said (John 6:51). The preacher must not approach the study of God's Word as mere academics or as a source for something to preach. It must be the means by which faith is kindled in his soul (Rom. 10:17).

Finally, fasting is a humbling discipline that brings greater focus to our walk with God. It crucifies the sensual aspects of our flesh. Admittedly the flesh does not cooperate easily with this discipline, but many preachers whose ministries have seen divine blessing joined fasting with their prayers: "This kind goeth not out but by prayer and fasting" (Matt. 17:21). John Wesley required his Methodist preachers to practice fasting twice a week.[5] How many Reformed men would qualify as Methodist lay preachers?

Many books have been written on spiritual disciplines. A preacher is not above his Lord, so we must follow in His steps. The Son of God practiced all the above disciplines, so what about us? We must prayerfully embrace these disciplines, remembering that the throne of grace has room for us. A new and living way has been opened, and God exhorts us to come boldly to find grace in our time of need (Heb. 4:16). Let us go and do likewise.

---

5. John Wesley was one of the primary preachers used by God (along with Whitefield) in the Great Awakening. While his soteriology was Arminian and therefore defective, he was a wonderful example of a disciplined open air preacher.

## Questions

1. How much time do you spend in prayer before you go out to preach?

2. How much time do you spend feeding on the Word of God each day? How can this time increase?

3. Is your meekness evident to all men, including the lost?

# Chapter Seven

# The Preacher's Competence

*Study to shew thyself approved unto God, a workman that needeth not to be ashamed, rightly dividing the word of truth.*
—2 Timothy 2:15

Imagine that you need open-heart surgery. Thankfully there are two surgeons available. The first surgeon is a Reformed Christian, a father of homeschoolers, perhaps even an elder in his church. He is well-liked by his neighbors and colleagues. He spends a week every year going on a mission trip and is very open about his faith. But only 50 percent of his patients survive his open-heart surgeries. The other doctor is an atheist. He swears at the nurses' station, belittles the Christian faith, and even kicks his dog when he gets home. Ninety-nine percent of his patients survive his open-heart surgeries. Which doctor will you prefer to do your surgery?

## Competence Matters

The truth is, competence matters. Providentially God has given many examples of competent evangelists throughout church history. Jesus, Peter, Paul, John Bunyan, and George Whitefield are a few examples. Jesus could preach standing up, sitting down, and while walking on the road. He could still the waves, give sight to the blind, and raise the dead. Even men sent to arrest Him said, "Never man spake like this man" (John 7:46). Jesus was not only the greatest preacher who ever lived, He was also the greatest teacher. Jesus outshines even the best of men as the sun outshines a candle. He was the master of illustrations and heuristic devices. He exemplified the highest levels of competence in His ministry. Peter too, filled with the Holy Ghost, preached a sermon that God used to bring three thousand souls to faith. Paul preached with competence, whether on Mars Hill or in front of the governor Festus. This is why we should ponder what constitutes competence as an open air preacher. We will look at this matter through three lenses: the preacher's method, message, and manner.

**The Method: Preach from the Bible**

Did Jesus have a method to His preaching? What about the apostle Paul? They did, and it was first and foremost to preach the Word of God. Jesus had an advantage we do not have. He was the Word and therefore was able to preach Himself. His first recorded sermon in Luke 4 is very instructive. Jesus read an Old Testament portion from Isaiah. He explained the text and how it pointed to Him. Then He made applications most of His listeners did not appreciate. They wanted to throw Him off a cliff!

If we are to imitate Jesus as open air preachers, we must preach that the Scriptures point to Christ. This involves knowing how to use any text to exalt Him, especially since all Scripture is about Him (Luke 24:27). The prince of preachers, Charles Spurgeon, described himself as a destination preacher: no matter where he was in the Bible, he always made a beeline to the cross! Similar to pulpit ministry, open air preaching should be text-driven. The difference is that the Scripture preached out in the open must be shorter and lend itself to an evangelistic call to repentance and faith in Christ. The preacher must select a text that can be explained succinctly and applied to the listeners in a direct, evangelistic way. This is why he must have a Bible in his hands while he preaches. How else will people know what you are doing while on the box or park bench? The Bible is our ultimate authority. People must see you are not preaching some ordinary message but one that comes from God as found in His Word.

Preaching from the text also keeps the open air preacher from rabbit trails and diversions. He will face plenty of distractions while preaching, and the text will keep him focused on where he is in the evangelistic sermon and where he wants to go. George Whitefield gives a more modern example of how to use Scripture skillfully in evangelism. He would read his text before preaching it, even though it was typically just one verse. Then he would extemporaneously preach the verse word by word, first through exposition, then application. He could tell hearers they were lost and hell-bound yet weep over their souls while doing so.[1]

## The Message: Ruin, Redemption, Regeneration

The preacher must remember that he has been entrusted with a message. He is to preach the very oracles of God (1 Peter 4:11). Paul said, "I determined not to know any thing among you, save Jesus Christ, and him crucified" (1 Cor. 2:2). Notice that Paul determined to know nothing else. He certainly could have illustrated Scripture by relying on his own intelligence or experiences, but instead he made Christ the center of his message. Likewise, we should concentrate on preaching the three Rs: ruin, redemption, and regeneration.[2] If we keep these three points in mind during every evangelistic message, there will be far less confusion among our hearers about why Jesus had to live a sinless life, die for our sins, and rise from the dead. We will also be far less prone to wander off into exposition on things that do not pertain to Christ: "Man's 'ruin' is the malady; 'redemption' and 'regeneration' are the remedy for man's sinful condition."[3]

Man's ruin in the fall and the holiness of God form the foundation of the message. It begins with God, whom Adam sinned against. Through one man's sin, we all fell and death entered the world (Rom. 5:12). We are under the sway of our fallen Adamic nature, in a spiritually ruined state, and unwilling to see the truth or come to the light. This reality of our guilt before God cannot be avoided. We preach about

---

1. George Whitefield was the greatest Reformed preacher of the eighteenth century. He was powerfully used by God as the means of many conversions during the Great Awakening.

2. These three aspects of a gospel sermon are taken from W. F. Bell, *Ruin, Redemption, Regeneration* (Pensacola, Fla.: Chapel Library, 2014).

3. Bell, *Ruin, Redemption, Regeneration*.

a Savior because men must be saved from their sin, their guilt, themselves, and, most importantly, from God's judgment.

Once the fall has been explained, the preacher needs to transition to redemption, or what God has done to open the way for sinners to be reconciled to Himself. God is the offended party, and only He knows what will appease His wrath and satisfy His justice. He must provide a plan of redemption, and that plan is wrapped up in the sinless life and substitutionary sacrifice of Jesus Christ. We are saved by His death and shed blood as a representative man, bearing the punishment for the sins of His people. In the Old Testament, animal sacrifice represented atonement for sin. Jesus was the Lamb of God sacrificed once for all, "the just for the unjust, that he might bring us to God" (1 Peter 3:18). Christ bore the full weight of God's wrath against His people on the cross so that "there is therefore now no condemnation to them which are in Christ Jesus" (Rom. 8:1).

We are also saved by the life of Christ. Imagine thirty-three years of trials and temptations. Why did Jesus have to live so long, face such hatred of the world, and be a man of sorrows and acquainted with grief? Because He was working out an impeccable righteousness as the last Adam, imputed to the benefit of His people: "For he hath made him to be sin for us, who knew no sin; that we might be made the righteousness of God in him" (2 Cor. 5:21). We have been declared righteous in Christ, to the praise of the glory of His grace!

Theologians speak of both the passive and active obedience of Christ. The active and passive obedience of Christ denote the dual aspect of what mankind needs. We need to have sin atoned for by a perfect sinless substitutionary sacrifice. God's fury must be assuaged. But we also need to have righteousness accredited to our account. These gifts come from Christ's active and passive obedience. God credits us with or imputes to us Christ's righteousness.

Just as we were ruined in the fall, and just as we are redeemed by the blood, so we also must be regenerated by the Spirit. Jesus taught Nicodemus that he must be born again (John 3). You must be born from above, or born of the Spirit, "for it is God which worketh in you both to will and to do of his good pleasure" (Phil. 2:13). Not only must our sins be atoned for but our evil hearts must be changed, which is why Peter said, "Being born again, not of corruptible seed, but of incorruptible, by the word of God, which liveth and abideth for ever" (1 Peter 1:23). God must not only satisfy His own perfect justice against sin but transform us from the inside out so we will love the things God loves and hate the things He hates. God must take out our evil hearts and replace them with ones that have been spiritually circumcised. Those whom God regenerates become "new creature[s]" (2 Cor. 5:17). Paul declared "the kingdom of God is…righteousness, and peace, and joy in the Holy Ghost" (Rom. 14:17). Unless we have been born again, we will never know the grace of imputed righteousness or the joy of having peace with God. Men cannot fix the mess they are in, nor do they want to!

We must also preach about repentance and faith in Jesus Christ. It is not enough to preach about Christ's death, burial, and resurrection. We must also tell our hearers how they are to respond to such a historical event. Repentance is turning away from sin, but the word also conveys a change of mind. Because the mind is the seat of action, when one's mind changes about God, actions will follow. Repentance is when a person loves or turns to the God he once hated, and hates or turns away from the sin he once loved. This is caused by a trust or belief in Christ, and specifically the promises and content about Him as found in the Scriptures. We must tell our hearers what it is to follow Christ, including the cost.

## The Preacher's Manner

The goal of pleasing God rather than man is a sobering endeavor. We have been entrusted with a message from the King and must therefore preach with authority. Jesus spoke and people marveled. He was not like the scribes and Pharisees. Our message is from God, and to reject it is to reject both Christ and God the Father. This is why there is no place for frivolity or silliness when preaching the gospel. People will be struck when your message is preached with authority. The Word carries its own weight, so explain absolute truth and apply it as something that is absolutely true! The best preachers are fervent in their preaching and have a certain unexplainable unction that is heaven-sent. They are wholeheartedly engaged in making much of Christ. Audiences take notice of preachers who have "been with Jesus" (Acts 4:13).

When the skeptical philosopher David Hume heard that George Whitefield was going to be preaching in his city, he decided to go hear him. Upon sharing his intentions with a friend, he was asked, "Surely you don't believe the things Whitefield preaches." Hume answered, "No, but Whitefield does." There is a magnetic attraction to a man wholeheartedly preaching Christ with authority. John Wesley also reportedly said that his method of preaching was to "light myself on fire, so people come to see me burn." To preach unenthusiastically is a sign of unbelief in the message. To speak in a monotone voice is perhaps proof you were not called to be an open air preacher.

When a man is filled with the life of God, a holy fire is kindled in his soul. Many times we have gone to preach at an abortion clinic dragging our feet. But when the Word begins to interact with our mind, whether through preaching or hearing others preach, there is a sense that God is owning His own Word, and fervency is affected. God is sending His Word out to accomplish His purposes, which are to convict, convert, or ultimately condemn. But God's Word is living and active, and so should be the preacher of it.

John Owen once made known his intention of traveling to hear John Bunyan preach. King Charles II was surprised that Owen, one of the brightest scholars in the British Empire, wanted to listen to a tinker's son. But Owen said, "May it please your Majesty, if I could possess the tinker's abilities to grip men's hearts, I would gladly give in exchange all my learning."[4]

Lastly, we must remember to have compassion for men. People are lost. They are sheep without a shepherd. Whitefield would shed tears as he pleaded with people to turn from their sins and come to Christ. People may hate your message, but they know when someone cares for them. We recall preaching one summer in a New York City park. One of the preachers stood at the microphone and patiently answered questions from the crowd. When a man came up and dumped water on the preacher, the crowd booed him for it. They did not like the preacher's message, but they could not deny he was treating them with respect

---

4. Adrian Warnock, "John Owen and Charles Spurgeon on John Bunyan," Patheos, October 24, 2007, http://www.patheos.com/blogs/adrianwarnock/2007/10/john-owen-and-charles-spurgeon-on-john/.

and affection. We are not Old Testament prophets. We are ambassadors of reconciliation. We owe no man anything but to love him with the gospel. Therefore we are to preach with authority and with affection for God and concern for men. We need to remember that when preaching in the open, most people's attention span is very short. But God's Word, preached by His servants, will not return void (Isa. 55:10–11). So preach expectantly, and let God give the increase (1 Cor. 3:7).

## Questions

1. Why would preaching with a Bible in your hand help to give authority to the message?

2. Would your listeners know you are zealous for Christ when you preach? Is there such a thing as being too zealous while preaching?

3. Does your preaching reach both mind and heart?

# Chapter Eight

# Response to Open Air Preaching

*And he said, Go, and tell this people, Hear ye indeed, but understand not; and see ye indeed, but perceive not.... Until the cities be wasted without inhabitant, and the houses without man, and the land be utterly desolate.*

—Isaiah 6:9, 11

The open air preacher will often be asked how many people he has led to Christ through his ministry. His answer should be, "All of them." Every time he preaches, if he is proclaiming the cross, people are led to Christ. What happens next is up to the Lord. This is why the gospel is always 100 percent effective. It always elicits a response. Some have ears to hear. Some gnash their teeth. Some walk past silently. Some leap and rejoice at the preaching of the gospel. But everyone responds. The gospel is never neutral or ineffective.

## Rejection to Be Expected

The cross of Christ has always been an offense to mankind, but this should never shut the mouth of the evangelist. Fiery trials will come against the one who publicly proclaims the gospel. The open air preacher must set his face like flint and plow on for the sake of his King. He must declare what "great things the Lord hath done" (Mark 5:19). There is a reason Paul was lashed 195 times, stoned once, beaten with rods on three different occasions, and was in danger from Jews, Gentiles, and false believers (2 Cor. 11:24–26). He opened his mouth about Christ in public and proclaimed the only way to God. The open air preacher must pray for strength to do the same. Recall the words of Jesus during His last supper with the disciples: "If the world hate you, ye know that it hated me before it hated you. If ye were of the world, the world would love his own: but because ye are not of the world, but I have chosen you out of the world, therefore the world hateth you. Remember the word that I said unto you, The servant is not greater than his lord. If they have persecuted me, they will also persecute you; if they have kept my saying, they will keep yours also" (John 15:18–20).

The preacher is promised suffering and the hatred of the world. More than this, and worst of all, the church or his family may even come against him. His flesh will come against him. The devil will come against him. He must set his face like flint (Isa. 50:7) and believe that the Lamb is worthy to suffer for.

The Scriptures promise that the world will see the preaching of the cross as "foolishness" (1 Cor. 1:18; 2:14). The street preacher will be viewed as "the savour of death" (2 Cor. 2:16), and this keeps many people from supporting his work. But he is the most privileged of all servants because he will see the promises of Scripture come to life every time he goes out. A putrefied corpse causes the face to scrunch up and the eyes to water. Mouths twist sideways when in the presence of death. People run away. The open air preacher sees these reactions every time he proclaims the gospel. Some people squint and holler. Many hurry past as rapidly as they can. He will seem ludicrous to the dying world. His message will be inane. It is exactly as the Scriptures say. But he must never forget it is "the foolishness of preaching" that the Lord uses to glorify His name and save sinners (1 Cor. 1:21).

## Professing Christians and Open Air Preaching

Atheists and nonbelievers are not the only ones who will come against the open air preacher. Professing Christians will come against him more than any other group. This is one of the most shocking and tragic realities that every public preacher faces. He must expect Christians to rebuke him for preaching in the open. Professing Christians are often the most persistent mockers of all. They will criticize him regardless of how or what he preaches. This is not to say that every Christian will have such a spirit. Many will come and thank him for preaching the cross. Many will shake his hand or bring him something to drink. But too many Christians will want to yank him down as ferociously as any atheist or Muslim.

This reaction to the public proclamation of the Word has been constant throughout history. The Old Testament prophets' worst foe was the religious establishment of the day. The same was true for Christ. The same happened to Whitefield and Wesley. Professing Christians will question the efficacy of the preaching. They will ask whether Jesus did it this way. They will tell the preacher he is not loving enough or he is too judgmental. They will say he is pushing sinners farther away. In every scenario the problem comes from the professing Christian not knowing or believing his Bible. Perhaps the professing Christian has never been born again and thus is no Christian at all. These kinds of grumblers will see the response of the unregenerate world. They will hear the scoffing. Then they will conclude, without their Bibles, that preaching in public must therefore be wrong. They will say it is harmful. But the preacher must stick to the Bible for his justification to preach in public, not the world or even the church in such instances. The Bible shows that this kind of response is expected from those dead in sin as well as professing Christians who have not submitted to the Scriptures in this area. It does not mean the preacher should intentionally antagonize others or look for such a response. He should never intentionally try to look foolish or provoke people's ire. But anyone faithfully proclaiming the Word of God will encounter a stiff-necked and adulterous generation and its typical responses.

It should go without saying, then, that the preacher should not expect any applause or appreciation from the people. This is what separates biblical evangelism from the seeker-friendly or friendship kinds. It is easy to take a lost person to supper or have them over for a barbecue. The lost will love you for it. There will be no offense or scandal. It is easy to bring lost people to a church filled with fog machines and carnal music and preaching that deals with social woes. It is easy to show a lost person the love of Jesus without ever opening your mouth about the exclusivity of His claims. Many in today's church hide behind these methods. Their chief desire is to look palatable in the eyes of sinners

(Gal. 1:10). Driven by fear of rejection, they do everything they can to tone down the affront of the cross, and so preach a different gospel altogether. That being said, it is important to note that relationships with the lost in order to bring them the gospel are perfectly biblical. A barbecue for the sake of the gospel is biblical. The point, however, is that the friendship or barbecue should not replace the gospel.

Seeker-friendly or friendship types of evangelism make the Christian feel good about his obedience to the Great Commission. He assumes he is doing his duty to the cause while at the same time preventing himself from appearing foolish or as "the savour of death" in the eyes of the unbeliever (2 Cor. 2:15–17). These kinds of craven methods emasculate the gospel and are not suitable for public preaching. A preacher must seek to be respectful and compassionate at all times, but he must never defang the offense of the cross. He must never be afraid of offending someone. The gospel is the power of God to salvation (Rom. 1:16), not barbecues or games or good manners.

This is why the open air preacher must expect opposition. "Jews require a sign, and the Greeks seek after wisdom," but the evangelist must "preach Christ crucified, unto the Jews a stumblingblock, and unto the Greeks foolishness" (1 Cor. 1:23). The majority of people exposed to the preaching of Christ will reject it before it reaches their ears. The seed will fall on hard ground (Matt. 13:1–23). The preacher who presents the beauty of Christ will discover that most are blind and unwilling to look on Him. This is why the professing Christian who does not know his Bible will see open air preaching as harmful or useless. But those who have studied the Bible, especially as it regards evangelism, will realize this kind of response corroborates perfectly with God's promise: "The natural man receiveth not the things of the Spirit of God: for they are foolishness unto him: neither can he know them, because they are spiritually discerned" (1 Cor. 2:14). Again, "If our gospel be hid, it is hid to them that are lost: in whom the god of this world hath blinded the minds of them which believe not, lest the light of the glorious gospel of Christ, who is the image of God, should shine unto them" (2 Cor. 4:3–4).

Man's greatest problem has always been pride festering in his heart, whether intellectual, physical, monetary, or spiritual. The cross directly confronts him at this point, which is why the cross will always appear foolish. Ancient Athens thought so. Modern college campuses think so. The unbelieving cousin or brother or parent thinks so. Even many churches think so. A preacher must never forget that the foolishness of preaching is what brings dead men to life. Softening the cross with clever speech or eloquence creates false converts who are drawn to cleverness or eloquence rather than Christ. Trying to meet the unbeliever on neutral ground can only lead to the further hardening of his heart, justifying his rebellion against God. The evangelist must proclaim Christ and Him crucified. He must stick to the foolishness of preaching and the gospel. God has always used humble means to save dead souls because in doing so He gets all the glory.

**Preaching at Different Venues**

The open air preacher must also keep in mind that responses differ depending on the venue. College campuses are vastly different from a downtown area. Festivals are different from sporting events. Abortion clinics are different from all of them. Being aware of each context is critical for the preacher. The gospel message should never change, but how people respond to it can be different in each scenario.

Preaching on a college campus will generally allow more interaction with the crowd than other places. Students will often gather around a preacher. Hecklers are certain. Because universities are steeped in liberalism, relativism, religious pluralism, Darwinian evolution, atheism, and sexual debauchery, the preaching of the cross will be loudly hailed as foolish, intolerant, and bigoted. Although the cross is certainly viewed this way in any setting, the campus is especially ideal for loud exchanges of opinion. Students usually have time to loiter. Many will have hours between classes. Frequently they will even skip class in order to heckle or hear the preacher. Many of the students will stand around and listen out of simple curiosity.

The evangelist's rights on college campuses are becoming squeezed more and more by college officials. It is a good idea to find out in advance what each campus allows. Each campus and state is different. Today most colleges restrict preaching to a "free speech zone." Most colleges will require a preacher to get permission in advance. Nevertheless, this remains one of the best mission fields in the country for an open air preacher. It is safe to say that most college students have never heard the true gospel.

The preacher visiting a college will discover that most campus ministries are dominated by friendship evangelism and will only rarely know what the true gospel is, much less appreciate your preaching it. Not offending the unbelieving students seems to be their primary objective. The open air preacher must be prepared to deal with criticism from the campus ministries. They are infamous for criticizing bold evangelism and will blame the preacher for hurting their ministries. They will claim that he talks too much about hell and that they must pick up the pieces after he leaves. Of course, heretical and hateful preachers do show up on campuses, so we should try to see this concern from the campus ministries' perspectives. Unfortunately the biblical preacher will often be clumped into the same category as those who preach harsh and legalistic doctrine. He cannot help this, but he can help the sad state of most campus ministries by simply engaging the students who are part of them. Talking to them about the gospel, about evangelism, and even about biblical conversion will perhaps help these kinds of Christians to see things in a different way.

Festivals and sporting events are alike in many ways. People are not prone to linger and listen to a word about God. Conversations will be more rare. Inebriation will be more common. The sports crowd is eager to get to the event. The festival crowd is anxious to be lost in debauchery. Tracts can be useful for such occasions. This is not to say that preaching in such venues is a wasted effort. On the contrary, it is necessary that the crowd's gaze should be lifted away from the things of the world at least for a moment. Amid such pomp and glitter, it is a privilege to hoist men's eyes to the things of God and eternal judgment. At the Super Bowl in San Francisco, two young men listened to us preach for hours before going into the game. They said they wanted to hear a word about God since it was Sunday. Similar to the campuses, it is important that the preacher knows where he is allowed to preach and which areas are restricted. A good rule of thumb is to find the ticket scalpers. They will not only be on public property but also know the heaviest areas of foot traffic.

Downtown crowds are generally in a hurry. They have errands to get done. They are on a limited lunch break. Most people will come across as apathetic. This should not discourage the preacher, since no one is apathetic to the cross. Preaching is never a waste of time. Every word of God will be to that person's salvation, sanctification, or condemnation. It does not return to Him void (Isa. 55:10–11). He is always glorified through the preaching of the cross. Downtown crowds may also be interspersed with the homeless population. In general the homeless will have a certain respect for the Word of God. Their response will usually be refreshing to the preacher. Something about the Son of God lightens the burden of the downcast and weary. Stoplight preaching should also not be overlooked. You will have only a couple of minutes, but preaching to the crowd as they wait to cross the street is an excellent way to get the gospel to stationary people. City courthouses are also good areas for a steady flow of foot traffic.

**Abortion Clinic Ministry**
Lastly, preachers should engage in ministry at abortion clinics whenever possible. This is a challenging venue. At the time of writing, close to 70 million abortions have taken place in America since 1973, which equates to almost a quarter of the entire US population. No one enjoys ministering at abortion clinics. It will always be a cross and will require self-denial and obedience to Christ. But the preacher must take the light of the gospel to the darkest spots on earth, and this is one of those places. It is shameful to think that Roman Catholics bring their beads and chants to the clinics far more often than the Protestant church brings the gospel.

Caution must be urged, however. What will stop abortion? It generally will not be preaching against abortion. The preaching of Jesus Christ saves sinners and, in the process, keeps their children from being killed. Even at abortion clinics, the name of Jesus Christ must ring forth more than any fact or proclamation about abortion. The best chance for a child to be saved from abortion is the child's mother or father being saved. As horrific as abortion statistics are (and it can be brought up when preaching), the power to save is in the gospel.

The intensity of preaching at an abortion clinic is indescribable. The stakes are tangible. Death is in the air, and the whole atmosphere reeks of murder. If a mother is willing to kill her child, why would she not kill a stranger, especially one calling her to repent? Although such a statement may sound extreme, anyone who has ministered at an abortion clinic for any length of time can attest to the regular threats and actual physical assaults that occur across America. These threats and assaults can also come from the father of the aborted child. Expect security guards and escorts that shuffle the mother into and out of the clinic. The gospel must go forth to these workers as well. Rage and tears will be a frequent sight. Remember that the mother knows that what she is doing is wrong. Her conscience is on your side. Use it as an ally. The preacher must keep a gentle, reasonable head. He must stick to the gospel of grace and forgiveness in Christ. Here more than anywhere else it is easy to get sidetracked into thinking the gospel is not enough. Here more than anywhere else it is easy to get carried away emotionally and respond in the flesh. But the gospel is what must be presented. The preacher will be nagged by his flesh to stay away. But here more than any other time he must crucify the flesh (Gal. 5:24), take up his cross, and go preach the gospel.

Abortion clinics can also be great places to evangelize to Roman Catholics. Although the primary focus should be preaching the gospel to the parents and guards at the clinic, it should be remembered that the veneration of Mary, the Mass, and many other doctrines held by the Roman Catholic Church are idolatrous. Roman Catholics are there because, at least in part, they believe doing so helps merit salvation. Many of them are just as undone by sin and tradition as the mothers killing their children or the guards and escorts who aid them. By all means, as occasion allows, share the gospel with them, but be careful not to get into arguments if unbelievers are listening. To the unknowledgeable person, this could come across as two Christians fighting each other.

—————————————— **Questions** ——————————————

1. Why do so many professing Christians see gospel preaching as offensive?

2. Besides the venues listed in this chapter, what other places might offer good opportunities for open air preaching?

3. Do you have a preaching venue to which you feel providentially called?

# Chapter Nine

# The Preacher's Response

*In the world ye shall have tribulation: but be of good cheer;
I have overcome the world.*

—John 16:33

If the entire world comes against the open air preacher—and at times it will seem like it—how should he respond? Proclaiming Christ in the midst of "wild beasts" on college campuses is not the most difficult task the preacher will face. Nor is it standing on a box in the middle of a gay pride parade and calling the lost to believe in Christ. It is responding to hostility and slander in the proper way.

## Jesus's, Peter's, and Paul's Responses to Hostility

Paul, Peter, and even our Lord provide lengthy discourses on the topic. Who better to provide authoritative exhortation on how we must respond to our worst foes? Our Lord was tempted in every way we are, yet was without sin (Heb. 4:15). He was threatened with stones, almost thrown off a cliff, and abandoned by disciples and family, yet He remained meek and lowly of heart (Matt. 11:29). Paul and Peter are some of the most passionate men presented to us in Scripture. Both were prone to fleshly responses. Both of them, ripened by the Holy Spirit, went on to exhort the Christian to put off such behavior.

Peter acknowledges that the Christian will suffer for the sake of righteousness (1 Peter 3:8–17). He even claims that by doing so he will "inherit a blessing." Peter encourages preachers to "be not afraid of their terror, neither be troubled; but sanctify the Lord God in your hearts."

He knew what it was to go into battle armed with the gospel. In the beginning he resorted to a literal, material sword against his enemies, hacking off ears without premeditation (John 18:10). His response to the Roman army must have been legendary since all the gospels contain it. Later in life, matured and battle-hardened, he went on to tell his readers to not render "evil for evil, or railing for railing: but contrariwise blessing; knowing that ye are thereunto called, that ye should inherit a blessing" (1 Peter 3:9). He must have learned such meekness from spending time before the Lord, not only while Christ was on earth but after His ascension as well. Consider again the words of Christ on the subject:

> But I say unto you which hear, Love your enemies, do good to them which hate you, Bless them that curse you, and pray for them which despitefully use you. And unto him that smiteth thee on the one cheek offer also the other; and him that taketh away thy cloak forbid not to take thy coat also…. But love ye your enemies, and do good, and lend, hoping for nothing again; and your reward shall be great, and ye shall be the children of the Highest: for he is kind unto the unthankful and to the evil. Be ye therefore merciful, as your Father also is merciful. (Luke 6:27–29, 35–36)

The open air preacher must defend the faith "with meekness and fear" (1 Peter 3:15), not bitterness or anger. He will be daily harassed by the world and professing Christians. He will be opposed by every crowd to whom he preaches. But he must always have in mind these words of Peter and Christ.

Paul also provides exhortation for preachers. A man of hot blood, he never flinched when harassed by opponents. Stoned at Lystra, he was dragged away as though dead (Acts 14:19–23). When he came to his senses, he did not stay down or walk away. He returned to the city. In Ephesus, Paul's companions had to hold him back from entering the theater when the city was in an uproar because of them (Acts 19:8–41). He was not one to avoid conflict, even opposing Peter to his face (Gal. 2:11–21). He was not ignorant of the preacher's battles: "When we were come into Macedonia, our flesh had no rest, but we were troubled on every side; without were fightings, within were fears" (2 Cor. 7:5). Yet later in his life Paul exhorts Timothy to be kind and gentle when dealing with opponents: "And the servant of the Lord must not strive; but be gentle unto all men, apt to teach, patient, in meekness instructing those that oppose themselves" (2 Tim. 2:24–25). Notice that Paul and Peter both employ the word *gentle*. These men were not effeminate. They were men's men. Yet they emphasize that the Christian must be gentle.

Paul goes a step further by saying "the servant of the Lord must not strive." Quarreling will be a constant temptation, as opponents will heckle a preacher in every way imaginable. Abuse will be thundered against the Lord's servant. Attacks and filthy words will be hurled against him. They may spit on him. They may throw coffee and beer and soda on him. They may yank the Bible from his hand and chew up the pages. Some may deck him in the jaw. Some may write defaming articles about him. But Paul says "be gentle unto all men." In his letter to the Romans he repeats the words of the Lord: "Bless them which persecute you; bless, and curse not" (Rom. 12:14). He exhorts the church to leave revenge to God and to overcome evil with good (Rom. 12:19). Paul exhorts the church in Colossae in a similar way: "Walk in wisdom toward them that are without, redeeming the time. Let your speech be always with grace, seasoned with salt, that ye may know how ye ought to answer every man" (Col. 4:5–6). In other words, an open air preacher must be kind, gentle, and wise toward his opponents every time he goes out, regardless of the circumstance.

Jesus also knew the preacher's battles. He was the greatest one to ever share God's Word. He knew the grind of heralding truth to all who have ears and to those who do not. Christ was fully God in every way as well as fully man. He was threatened with stones, false accusations, mobs who tried to kill Him, and the devil. He was betrayed by family, by disciples, by the religious establishment, and by His own nation, yet He commands His preachers, "Love your enemies, do good to them which hate you, bless them that curse you, and pray for them which despitefully use you" (Luke 6:27–28).

The preacher does well to proclaim the gospel in the highways and hedges. But is he obedient to the more difficult task of loving his enemy or doing good to those who hate him? Does he bless those who curse him and pray for those who mistreat him? Jesus asked His disciples, "Why call ye me, Lord, Lord, and do not the things which I say?"

(Luke 6:46). The same could be said for the preacher who responds to his opponents with the wrong spirit. He will be proclaiming the gospel to people whose father is "the devil" (John 8:44–45), and they will announce themselves as his enemy in every way they can. A preacher must expect it. But how will he respond? "If any man among you seem to be religious, and bridleth not his tongue, but deceiveth his own heart, this man's religion is vain" (James 1:26). A man does well to preach the gospel on the streets, but only to the extent he responds to the lost in the right way.

### Exemplary Responses to Evil from Church History

Examples abound in church history of open air preachers responding both correctly and incorrectly to opposition. Studying these men can be a great encouragement and refiner for the evangelist. Consider the following about John Furz, an eighteenth-century open air preacher: "As soon as I began to preach, a man came straight forward, and presented a gun at my face; swearing that he would blow my brains out, if I spake another word. However, I continued speaking, and he continued swearing, sometimes putting the muzzle of the gun to my mouth, sometimes against my ear. While we were singing the last hymn, he got behind me, fired the gun, and burned off part of my hair."[1]

Such an experience is not novel when it comes to open air preaching. In his book *Evangelism in the Early Church*, Michael Green demonstrates again and again that public preaching brought the same response in the first two centuries as it does today: "The mockery, the joking, the heckling, even the physical danger to the preacher which he describes must have happened on countless open air platforms."[2] Historian Ramsay MacMullen documents the same thing: "Even Paul and his fellow preachers had found it, or rather their words had made it, a dangerous business."[3]

---

1. Thomas Jackson, ed., *The Lives of Early Methodist Preachers* (London: Wesleyan Conference Office, 1873), 125.
2. Green, *Evangelism in the Early Church*, 306.
3. Ramsay MacMullen, *Christianizing the Roman Empire* (New Haven, Conn.: Yale University Press, 1984), 105.

This is why incidents such as the following from the eighteenth century should not surprise us, other than their Spirit-filled responses. John Nelson recounts,

> When I was in the middle of my discourse, one at the outside of the congregation threw a stone, which cut me on the head: however that made the people give greater attention, especially when they saw the blood run down my face; so that all was quiet till I had done, and was singing a hymn.[4]

As for Daniel Rowland,

> It was understood he was to preach in the open air, and one vicious man prepared a great amount of gunpowder under the spot where he and his congregation were to gather, and with a thin line of powder from the store to some distance away, where it ended in a pile of straw. The aim was to fire the straw and blow up the preacher and his hearers. Providentially, someone arrived at the scene before the service began and discovered the plot. In almost every place, he was in danger of abuse unless he stopped his work. Howell Harris wrote to Whitefield on 1 March 1743: "Brother Rowland had a little interruption a fortnight ago by some drunkards, but God fills his soul sweetly."[5]

Unless these men stopped preaching, the danger would continue, but they never stopped, and neither should we. The hope and prayer of every open air preacher should not be "Lord keep me from danger" but rather "Lord, when danger comes, fill my soul 'sweetly' with your Spirit."

These examples demonstrate why the open air preacher must guard against a bitter spirit. He will engage the worst demons in the world, and preaching to the lost can make the most mature hearts callous and numb even the most compassionate of preachers. His awareness of the danger will help him to be constant in prayer against such deadening, poisonous effects. Like all the most heinous sins, bitterness takes place slowly. The preacher will not wake up one morning and suddenly be bitter toward the lost. In the beginning, most preachers will be tender

---

4. John Nelson, as quoted in Spurgeon, *Lectures to My Students*, 125.
5. Jones and Morgan, *Calvinistic Methodist Fathers*, 78–79.

and patient. They will reason with the lost like a mother dealing with a child. But slowly the patience wanes. Each day the preacher is cloaked with a thin sheet of resentment. The blasphemies of the lost begin to wear on him. Eventually he sees them through a lens of burning hatred rather than love. He forgets that apart from the grace of God he would be just as lost. He gets to the point that he is no longer concerned about their souls. He sees preaching as a duty, something to check off the list, not as good news for sinners. This happens unconsciously. The preacher likely will never notice it, and this is the danger. This is why he needs to be held accountable to his church and other brothers. In some cases, even if he does become aware of it, his hatred and bitterness for the lost will be so great that it will not bother him. He will blame the lost rather than repent and ask God for more tenderness. This is a danger for every open air preacher. He is constantly battling the evils of this world and dealing with people who hate him and hate God. He must constantly examine himself and be the most prayerful saint in the city.

Robert Flockhart of Edinburgh was known for his fiery temperament, yet consider Spurgeon's description of him:

> Though a lesser light, he was a constant one, and a fit example to the bulk of Christ's street witnesses. Every evening, in all weathers and amid many persecutions, did this brave man continue to speak in the street for forty-three years. Think of that, and never be discouraged. When he was tottering to the grave the old soldier was still at his post. "Compassion to the souls of men drove me," said he, "to the streets and lanes of my native city, to plead with sinners and persuade them to come to Jesus. The love of Christ constrained me."[6]

A preacher must pray for such love. The natural man cannot do it because his flesh will not allow it. But "greater is he that is in you, than he that is in the world" (1 John 4:4).

## How to Respond to Police and Authorities

The open air preacher is required by God to be "subject unto the higher powers" (Rom. 13:1). It is no coincidence these words were written to

---

6. Spurgeon, *Lectures to My Students*, 125.

believers in Rome at the height of emperor worship and other pagan rituals. The open air preacher must not resist the governing authorities, since doing so would be to resist the authorities who "are ordained of God" to bear the sword (Rom. 13:1). But notice that Paul's argument pivots on the assumption that the governing authorities "are not a terror to good works, but to the evil" (Rom. 13:3). So what happens when the governing authorities do become terrors to good works or good behavior as outlined in Scripture? What happens when the governing authorities attempt to stop someone from preaching the gospel in public, ostensibly for the sake of appeasing the desires of a rebellious nation? Paul says the authorities bear the sword for the purpose of carrying out God's wrath "upon him that doeth evil" (Rom. 13:4). What happens when the sword comes against those preaching Christ? What happens when a preacher is treated as the wrongdoer simply because he is opening his mouth about God in public? Surely there is a perversion of justice in this case. But how should the preacher respond?

We hesitate to appeal to the United States Constitution and the protection it promises under the First Amendment, because the preacher will encounter police officers and a public who no longer cherish or give authority to the Constitution. It is true that the preacher should be protected by it in most cases. It is also true that, if the current trends continue, he will not be. The rights of the open air preacher are being pushed into irrelevancy. His voice is being quieted. Even public areas such as downtown centers or city sidewalks now come with restrictions such as decibel limits or amplification laws. The freedom to preach in public is slowly being eliminated in America and the United Kingdom, among other places. So what should the preacher do? Would resisting such rules go against Paul's commands in Romans 13? Are there times when defying authority is not only acceptable but even required of the evangelist? Is the maxim true that whenever preaching is outlawed, only the outlaws will preach?

First of all, our authority for preaching the gospel comes from Christ, not the government. All authority in the universe belongs to Christ, who has told us to bring the gospel to a lost world. We hold that a preacher should be respectful at all times to the governing authorities, insofar as they are human beings and made in the image of God. If he is to be arrested, let him conduct himself with gentleness and respect. If he is to defy authorities, let him do so with all the meekness of Jesus, who "afflicted, yet he opened not his mouth: he is brought as a lamb to the slaughter, and as a sheep before her shearers is dumb, so he openeth not his mouth" (Isa. 53:7). The preacher should never intentionally provoke the authorities for the sake of being arrested or any other purpose. But we believe that caving to the perversion of justice or the corruption of a country's agenda against God is likewise unbiblical. We are told to preach the gospel to all creation (Mark 16:15). If a man is arrested for preaching, he follows others who have been similarly treated, including the apostle Paul, who wrote Romans 13. In such a case he should not be ashamed.

The New Testament church in a sense was founded by preachers who were regularly arrested. Consider Peter and John in the early part of Acts: "And as they spake unto the people, the priests, and the captain of the temple, and the Sadducees, came upon them, being grieved that they taught the people, and preached through Jesus the resurrection from the dead. And they laid hands on them, and put them in hold unto the next day: for it was now eventide" (Acts 4:1–3).

Note that the officials were grieved because they were teaching the people and proclaiming Jesus. Let this be the reason the preacher is arrested, if any. This proclamation was what antagonized the officials, not a social agenda. Afterward when Peter and John were told to stop preaching Christ, they declined to obey: "Whether it be right in the sight of God to hearken unto you more than unto God, judge ye. For we cannot but speak the things which we have seen and heard" (Acts 4:19–20). Rather than being daunted by public officials and criticism from the community, they went on to pray for increased boldness: "Now, Lord, behold their threatenings: and grant unto thy servants, that with all boldness they may speak thy word" (Acts 4:29). Likewise, the preacher should preach the cross without fear of public officials or concern for his well-being. He should proclaim Christ and Him crucified until the whole world either comes against him or is saved.

One chapter later the apostles are arrested again. Far from submitting to unlawful authorities, they escape from jail after God Himself sends an angel to deliver them. The angel commands them to "Go, stand

and speak in the temple to the people all the words of this life. And when they heard that, they entered into the temple early in the morning, and taught" (Acts 5:20–21). Again the apostles are arrested and are told to stop preaching by the authorities. Again the apostles defy this command: "Then Peter and the other apostles answered and said, We ought to obey God rather than men" (Acts 5:29). Peter goes on to preach Christ to the officials, and the response is starkly familiar to what many open air preachers receive today: "When they heard that, they were cut to the heart, and took counsel to slay them" (Acts 5:33). Church history tells us that eventually these men were killed. Stephen is killed two chapters later for openly preaching Christ, which is a reminder that the church was built by the blood and, to a degree, unlawful arrests of preachers. We saw earlier that the church father Cyprian, also an open air preacher, "even dared the authorities to arrest him as he preached in the market place during a period of persecution."[7] Although we would not encourage such an act, we can appreciate his bold insight into the conflict between gospel preaching and most governments.

At the end of the day, the more people who hear the gospel, the better. When a preacher is arrested, he should proclaim Christ in jail. He should preach Christ to all who have ears. Decades of compromise to unlawful authorities have greatly reduced the rights of the evangelist in the West. But he must never stop preaching just because it is illegal or distasteful to the culture. When preaching is outlawed—and it will be—he "ought to obey God rather than men" (Acts 5:29).

---

7. Green, *Evangelism in the Early Church*, 304.

## Questions

1. When a preacher responds to an unbeliever in a manner according to the flesh, should he apologize?

2. How can an open air preacher protect himself from unlawful arrests or accusations?

3. Do you believe and practice the proverb, "A soft answer turneth away wrath" (Prov. 15:1)?

*Chapter Ten*

# Exhortation to the Church and Seminaries

*One of the laws of the Presbytery of Glasgow is that every minister, once a month, shall obey the command of the Lord Jesus Christ and "go out into the highways and the hedges and compel sinners to come in."… I think this would be a good thing for all our Theological Seminaries, our Bible Institutes, our Training Schools for Christian work to insist on.*

—William Evans, *Open Air Preaching*

It is hard to be an open air preacher, and being Reformed makes it even harder. We are told not to be surprised if the world hates us as Christians (1 John 3:13), and we should expect it to hate us even more if we preach the gospel in public. Yet the disdain professing Christians have toward intentional, frontline gospel preaching is a surprise. Consider again what evangelist Al Baker has observed on the topic: "Many of the leading pastors of our day reject out of hand direct, intentional, bold evangelistic outreach. They tend to over-contextualize the gospel message when in the midst of atheists, agnostics, and militant unbelievers…. And what's behind this approach is the convinced position by many that direct, bold, intentional, Scripture-saturated evangelism simply does not work in our postmodern world."[1]

---

1. Baker, "Three Reasons Why We Need Evangelists."

## Charting a Way Forward for Open Air Preaching

Open air evangelists are frontline ministers. When called to move from the pew to the streets or from the safety of the study to the carnage of battle, few Christians will join in. To see the works of the Lord, one must set out for deep waters (Ps. 107), but sadly very few in Christ's body are willing to do so, much less support the ones who do. The loss to the church is immeasurable.

Our goal in this chapter is not to curse the darkness, but to light a candle.[2] The open air preacher should not be insecure about his calling or occupied with approbation from others. It is a great privilege to experience some of the rejection Jesus experienced, even if it comes in large part from professing Christians. Preachers should be mindful that every unkind word and rejection is a reason to "rejoice" and "leap for joy: for, behold, your reward is great in heaven" (Luke 6:23). He should carry a compassionate pity for the bulk of Christians who have questioned the efficacy of open air preaching without any real battle experience. The Lord is "a very present help in trouble" (Ps. 46:1), but especially when such trouble is experienced when striving for His glory.

Before charting out a way for preachers to interact with fellow believers on the topic, it is salutary to issue a warning: do not get your hopes up that ministers, seminarians, or individual Christians will be very interested in your calling or in open air preaching in general. Such a statement is not meant to be an overt attack against such people, but rather a way to protect the evangelist from unrealistic expectations. Paul, one of the greatest preachers in church history, said that God has set apart apostles as "the filth of the world…the offscouring of all things" (1 Cor. 4:13). Many of his critics were fellow believers and leaders, some of whom were converted under his preaching. If this is how they treated Paul, then today's open air preacher must expect it as well. If you are truly called to be such a minister, you are going to experience rejection by many in the Christian community.

---

2. This phrase is generally attributed to an early twentieth-century preacher named William Watkinson.

**The Causes of Rejection from Professing Christians**

A number of explanations have already been offered for why professing Christians so often reject us. We will now consider a few more. Many church leaders are unwilling to take up their cross, deny the rejection of the world, and make an open stand for Christ. Consequently, they will not lead others onto the battlefield. Churches are filled with leaders who have time for golf and luncheons but no time for evangelism. The flesh, which cries out to be spared embarrassment, is not mortified, even though this is precisely the path to Christian maturity. Unless God is earnestly sought in prayer, man's default will always be to spare the flesh and avoid anything that might wage war against it.

The leadership's lack of zeal for the battle ensures that individual Christians will remain spiritual weaklings. Instead of the church militant, we have become the church recumbent. No wonder the world has no fear of the church. Most churches want easy ministries such as feeding the homeless or friendship evangelism. The homeless do not give Christians much trouble when getting free food. Handing out water bottles with church invitations will not encounter many difficulties. But then again, that is not gospel preaching.

One time we brought a young man to downtown Raleigh to train him in open air preaching. Homeless people were lined up to get food, making for a great audience. One of the preachers set up the box by the sidewalk and greeted the crowd, saying he was there to feed them the Word of God. The homeless received the Word with joy, but the supposed minister who was overseeing the food ministry yelled out, "We don't preach to the people!" He insisted that the preacher stop. But dealing with such objections was part of the training program, so the preacher continued. The man who objected called the police, but when the officers came out and heard his complaints, they simply walked away.

Another time, one of us was preaching in front of the Orlando Magic's basketball arena. A man was offended when hearing that abortion is murder and that "all murderers would have their place in the lake of fire." He denounced the preacher in front of the crowd, saying, "The Bible doesn't teach that," and continued, "As a seminary professor and ordained minister, I know better than you!" The Scriptures tell us that the devil disguises himself as an angel of light (2 Cor. 11:14), and it was likely so in this case. Even some seminarians and clergy exhibit a cultural bias against open air preaching, just as in the days of Jesus, Paul, and George Whitefield.

Besides the ingrained bias against public evangelism, people wish to avoid conflict at all costs, and open air preaching is often bound up in conflict. But this fleshly reaction profits nothing. The uncrucified flesh will not cooperate with activities done in the power of the Spirit. If ministers will not anticipate this enemy within themselves, they will not be able to instruct their flock about the necessary resistance against the flesh when reaching out with the gospel. It is this knowledge of indwelling corruption that makes a man rush boldly to God for strength and power in the midst of battle: "Fear of man bringeth a snare" (Prov. 29:25).

Preaching that confronts sin and commands repentance will be met by audiences that react. This sometimes causes a Christian to disbelieve the necessity or efficacy of such evangelism. But what else should we expect when bringing the gospel of light to the darkness? People reacted in three ways when Paul preached (Acts 17). Some sneered. Others wanted to hear him again. And some believed and followed Christ. Those are always the reactions to the preaching of God's Word. Why do people consider the sneering of the lost as though "some strange thing happened unto you" (1 Peter 4:12) or as though the evangelism must be unsuccessful on account of it? Where are those "who by reason of use have their senses exercised to discern both good and evil" (Heb. 5:14)?

Many clergymen and Christians diminish and even criticize the open air preacher because they are convicted of their own lack of faithfulness in this area. Paul told Timothy to "do the work of an evangelist" (2 Tim. 4:5). As a pastor, Timothy was exhorted to discharge all the duties of his ministry, including evangelism. Paul would rebuke many ministers today not only for what they preach but for where they fail to preach. The gospel must be preached outside church walls—and not only by the open air preacher! Spurgeon said a minister would have a hard time making the defense that he has fulfilled his duties by preaching once a week in the church.[3] This is why evangelism must be a scheduled discipline, especially by the ministers of a flock. The sowing of gospel seeds must be scheduled and obeyed, not left to feelings. Most ministers

---

3. Spurgeon, *Lectures to My Students*, 254.

find time to schedule meetings with elders, meetings about the budget, and meetings about meetings, but if a minister refuses to make soul winning part of his schedule, is he not being faithful to his calling?

We are convinced this antipathy toward open air preaching can be corrected by changing the culture toward biblical evangelism. A complete overhaul of methods such as friendship evangelism and secular methodologies is a must. The Reformed churches must return to simple gospel preaching and prayer, relying on God alone to give the increase. A change is needed not only for the sake of the lost outside the church but for genuine Christians as well. The salubrious effects of bold, frontline evangelism on laymen are impossible to underestimate.

**Open Air Preaching Must Be Reassessed at the Seminary Level**
Biblical evangelism must be promoted and led by the ministers, although it should begin at the seminary level, when future ministers are in their formative years. This is why we believe the path forward starts at seminary. Many Reformed seminaries include an evangelism course. This is to be commended, but most courses encourage only one-on-one evangelism. This would be fine for laymen but not for preachers of the gospel. A future minister should be engaged in one-on-one evangelism already; otherwise he should not be studying for the ministry. What is needed is more evangelistic preaching done outside church walls, far away from the comfort of any pulpit. Aside from the unique challenges that open air preaching provides the seminarian, it will cause him to overcome fears of man and the flesh, which will greatly help him years later when settling into a pulpit ministry. We understand that most pulpit ministers will not be evangelists. But once future ministers are exposed to street evangelism, they will understand the biblical mandate for its practice and become better preachers for doing it.

One year, for instance, Reformed Theological Seminary–Charlotte allowed a group of open air preachers to host a pizza luncheon for the seminarians. After speaking to the group on street evangelism, two men became committed to it on a weekly basis in the Charlotte area. A group of open air preachers was also received by Puritan Reformed Theological Seminary, under the leadership of Dr. Joel Beeke. After chapel exhortations on Reformed evangelism, several future ministers joined the preachers on the streets of Grand Rapids for intentional open air preaching. Keeping the students engaged in such evangelism requires leadership and commitment from the seminary. Weekly or monthly evangelism should become part of the curriculum! According to William Evans, a preacher from the early twentieth century, "One of the laws of the Presbytery of Glasgow is that every minister, once a month, shall obey the command of the Lord Jesus Christ and 'go out into the highways and the hedges and compel sinners to come in.'" He went on to suggest, as we do, "I think this would be a good thing for all our Theological Seminaries, our Bible Institutes, our Training Schools for Christian work to insist on...that a place shall be provided in their faculties for a teacher and professor of open air work; and that it shall be considered a part of the training of every student for the ministry of the gospel of Jesus Christ."[4]

To achieve a widespread impact on church and culture, open air evangelism must become part of the seminary curriculum—not a small reference in a particular course of study but an actual weekly or at least monthly prerogative that takes the gospel outside the church and seminary. Christianity needs men who "preach the word...in season, out of season" (2 Tim. 4:2). If seminaries intentionally move future ministers out of the classroom and onto the battlefield, there is hope that ministers will be better able to envision how Jesus trained His disciples. If seminaries want to launch evangelistic leaders into the churches worldwide, then they must mobilize their students to the front lines with the gospel. After all, seminaries should be places where soldiers get training in all spheres of the battle. It is much too easy to hide in libraries for four years and turn out nothing but ivory-tower soldiers. You cannot plow a field by turning it over in your mind—action must be taken! Seminaries must become the proving ground not only for whether a minister can write an essay or read certain theologians, but for whether the preacher is willing to crucify the flesh and herald the Word in public. Seminaries must become boot camps intent on sending soldiers into battle who know how to overcome the enemy by the "word of their testimony" (Rev. 12:11)!

---

4. Evans, *Open Air Preaching*, 8.

We by no means discourage seminary training. Ministers and the church tend to recognize advanced degrees as the "union card" of our day. Every open air preacher would do well to pursue some kind of formal education from doctrinally sound seminaries if possible. Aside from the theological help this would provide, this would equip both the open air preacher and pulpit ministers with a shared educational background and possibly more open doors for the evangelist as it regards the church. If churches and seminaries are going to warm up to open air preaching, then preachers must look into taking this step. It would be great if more ministers were friends with such preachers and even had them on their staff. As evangelists, we must make the effort to be team players and valued members of the church. The more well-studied the open air preacher, the better he will be in his calling and the more likely he will be to get a hearing in the seminaries and churches.

A balanced church will incorporate the evangelist into its leadership. If such a paradigm were emphasized at seminaries, future ministers would be more likely to act on it. For example, one Presbyterian church in Florida had been praying that God would send them an evangelist. Unknown to them, open air preacher Jimbo Mullen was praying for a church that understood his calling as an evangelist. The Lord brought the two together. Now their relationship has developed so nicely that the church has put up Jimbo's family in the parsonage. This is the fruit of incorporating the evangelist into the life of the church.

Jimmy Hamilton, a UK Presbyterian pastor for more than twenty years (known in England as "The Street Preacher"), said this about the current relationship between open air preachers and church leadership:

> Preaching the gospel on the streets is a ministry that few Pastors or Christians would dare support. Sadly many Pastors and Christians do nothing but complain and criticize open air preachers. But here's the thing, in the UK and America, since the Reformation days, we've had guys like this wandering around our cities and towns preaching the gospel to a nation of ruined sinners. It's part of our great evangelical heritage. Men whose shoelaces this generation is not fit to loose. We love the local church and its incumbent Minister, and we would love their support, IF ONLY....
> But we realize most churches don't want to be disturbed, don't understand us, that we even scare some. But just like God called

you to do what you've got to do, so God called us to do what we do.... It saddens me that with the powers of the world and hell set against Christians in our land today, open air preachers find ourselves being picked at by those who ought to stand alongside us. I believe with the apostate condition the visible church is in, in our land today, she is in no place to criticize the open air preacher: "Physician, heal thyself." Instead of criticizing us, pray for us and for yourself.... But be warned, God answers prayer.[5]

We are not arguing that all Christians must preach in public. But a healthy church sends its people to the streets as part of its evangelistic duties. While the open air preacher addresses the crowd with God's Word, individual members can pray or distribute tracts, leading to meaningful one-to-one gospel conversations. Christ's church is healthiest when the body is active outside the church. If any church or seminary is seeking help in this area, we regularly hold conferences and training for the sake of mobilizing Christians and churches to get onto the streets with the gospel. Once ministers and theologians enlist for the battle, other Christians will join the fight. The prayer meetings will be more zealous. The Bible studies will be more meaningful. The evangelism done in private spheres will become more routine and fruitful. Everyone in the church benefits when the body is engaged in intentional, bold, frontline evangelism. May the Lord give us all the grace to be more faithful to our call.

---

5. Personal correspondence with the author.

## Questions

1. Open air preacher, are you willing to get advanced theological education if it means having a greater impact on the work?

2. Pastor, teacher, or professor, are you willing to lead an evangelistic team to the streets in conjunction with your regular ministry duties?

3. Open air preacher and pastor, are you willing to learn from others who are perhaps more evangelistically gifted than you?

# Conclusion: Heard the Call?

*In what place therefore ye hear the sound of the trumpet,
resort ye thither unto us: our God shall fight for us.*
—Nehemiah 4:20

Orthodoxy and orthopraxy are essential for open air preaching. To know you are being called to preach in this way is great. To be approved in this calling is even better. If you are sensing a call to preach, seek other experienced ministers (preferably from your church) to mentor you and give you feedback on your giftedness. Remember, there is no rush. Paul told Timothy, "Lay hands suddenly on no man" (1 Tim. 5:22). While there is a great need in our culture and country for Reformed evangelists, God's timing is perfect. Test your internal call and ask for input and critique to see if there is also an external call, or confirmation from other mature men.

If you are convinced that God is calling you to open air preaching, the next step is to prepare. You must "study to show thyself approved unto God, a workman that needeth not to be ashamed, rightly dividing the word of truth" (2 Tim. 2:15). You must "meditate upon these things; give thyself wholly to them; that thy profiting may appear to all" (1 Tim. 4:15). Solomon said, "Seest thou a man diligent in his business? he shall stand before kings; he shall not stand before mean men" (Prov. 22:29). It is doubtful the evangelist will stand before kings, but the verse encourages any Christian to be skilled in their work, which includes the task of public preaching. Along with studying the Scriptures, the preacher should study doctrine and church history. He must be a theologian, not only for the sake of better expounding the Word of God but, most importantly, for the sake of knowing God better. Work on your preaching by preaching. Get out and actually do it. As much as is humanly possible, never turn down an opportunity to preach unless the Lord expressly forbids it. Spend time on your knees. The open air preacher must spend as much time praying as he does preaching, remembering that "when thou prayest, enter into thy closet, and when thou hast shut thy door, pray to thy Father which is in secret; and thy Father which seeth in secret shall reward thee openly" (Matt. 6:6).

Also remember that you are called to preach the oracles of God, not politics or some pet issue. Many preachers are tempted to proclaim themselves or their denominations, but we are called to preach Christ: His person, work, resurrection, ascension, and the call to repent and believe the gospel. We must preach the holiness of God and all that it entails. We must preach the Scriptures, "For after that in the wisdom of God the world by wisdom knew not God, it pleased God by the foolishness of preaching to save them that believe" (1 Cor. 1:21).

The trumpet has blown, dear preacher—did you hear it? A clarion call to the battle! So go forth and battle, not using the flesh or the weapons of the world, but the weapons of God, which are "mighty through God to the pulling down of strong holds" (2 Cor. 10:4). Battle boldly, not hiding the offense of the cross. Preach boldly that men must repent or perish. The natural man is always unwilling to be saved, but God has mercy "on whom I will have mercy, and I will have compassion on whom I will have compassion" (Rom. 9:15). Our job is to preach the cross, knowing that God alone causes the increase (1 Cor. 3:7). All whom the Father has given the Son will come to Him (John 6:37), so preach Christ in season and out of season (2 Tim. 4:2). Go forth to preach His sinless life and atoning death in the streets, at the abortion clinic, on the campus, in front of the stadiums, at the local fair, and wherever else you find a heap of souls dithering about in their daily concerns. Preach Jesus Christ, a great Savior for sinners, "a name which is above every name" (Phil. 2:9). Make much of Christ, preacher! Men must call on His name in order to be saved. "He that hath ears to hear, let him hear" (Matt. 11:15).

# Bibliography

Bahnsen, Greg. *Van Til's Apologetic*. Phillipsburg, N.J.: P&R Publishing, 1998.

Baker, Al. "Three Reasons Why We Need Evangelists." Banner of Truth. October 23, 2017. https://banneroftruth.org/us/resources/articles/2017/three-reasons-need-evangelists/?utm_content=bufferb 6c11&utm_medium=social&utm_source=facebook.com&utm _campaign=buffer.

Beeke, Joel. *Puritan Evangelism*. Grand Rapids: Reformation Heritage Books, 2007.

Bell, W. F. *Ruin, Redemption, Regeneration*. Pensacola, Fla.: Chapel Library, 2014.

Bonar, Horatius. *True Revival*. Pensacola, Fla.: Chapel Library, 2000.

Buettel, Cameron. "Cameron Buettel Interviews Paul Washer." Sermon Audio. July 23, 2009. https://www.sermonaudio.com/sermoninfo .asp?m=t&s=723091214300.

Byington, Edwin. *Open-Air Preaching: A Practical Manual for Pastors, Evangelists, and Other Christian Workers*. Hartford, Conn.: Hartford Theological Seminary, 1892.

Calvin, John. *Institutes of the Christian Religion*. Edited by John McNeill. Louisville, Ky.: Westminster Press, 1960.

Charmley, Gervase N. "John Knox: The Making of a Reformer." Banner of Truth, October 21, 2015. https://banneroftruth.org/us /resources/articles/2015/john-knox-the-making-of-a-reformer/.

Dallimore, Arnold. *George Whitfield: God's Anointed Servant*. Wheaton, Ill.: Crossway, 1990.

————. *George Whitefield: The Life and Times of the Great Evangelist of the Eighteenth-Century Revival*. Vol. 1. Carlisle, Pa.: Banner of Truth, 1970.

Evans, William. *Open Air Preaching*. New York: Fleming H. Revell, 1901.

EWTN. "St. Francis of Assisi: Founder of the Franciscan Order." Accessed May 25, 2018. http://www.ewtn.com/saintsHoly/saints /F/stfrancisofassisi.asp.

Flockhart, Robert. *The Street Preacher*. Grand Rapids: Baker, 1977.

Gairdner, James. *Lollardy and the Reformation in England: An Historical Survey*. Vol. 2. London: Macmillan, 1908.

Glinney, Edward, ed. *Missions in a New Millennium*. Grand Rapids: Kregel Publications, 2000.

Green, Michael. *Evangelism in the Early Church*. Grand Rapids: Eerdmans, 1970.

Gurnall, William. *The Christian in Complete Armour*. 1662. Reprint, London: Banner of Truth, 1964.

Hernandez, Sonny. *Apologetics Primer for the Armed Forces*. Clarksville, Tenn.: Reforming America Ministries, 2017.

Jackson, Thomas, ed. *The Lives of Early Methodist Preachers*. London: Wesleyan Conference Office, 1873.

Jones, John Morgan, and William Morgan. *The Calvinistic Methodist Fathers of Wales*. Vol. 1. 1890. Reprint, Carlisle, Pa.: Banner of Truth, 2016.

Larsen, David L. *The Company of the Preachers*. Grand Rapids: Kregel Publications, 1998.

Lloyd-Jones, D. M. *Romans, Exposition of Chapters 7.1–8.4*. Carlisle, Pa.: Banner of Truth, 1973.

MacMullen, Ramsay. *Christianizing the Roman Empire*. New Haven, Conn.: Yale University Press, 1984.

Murray, Iain. *Revival and Revivalism*. Carlisle, Pa.: Banner of Truth, 1994.

Nichols, Stephen J., ed. *Martin Luther's Ninety-Five Theses*. Phillipsburg, N.J.: P&R Publishing, 2002.

Owen, John. *The Glory of Christ*. 1850. Reprint, Carlisle, Pa.: Banner of Truth, 1965.

Packer, J. I. *Evangelism and the Sovereignty of God.* Nottingham, England: Inter-Varsity Press, 2008.

Sproul, R. C. *The Consequences of Ideas: Understanding the Concepts That Shaped Our World.* Wheaton, Ill.: Crossway, 2000.

———. *Essential Truths of the Christian Faith.* Carol Stream, Ill.: Tyndale House, 1992.

Spurgeon, Charles. *Lectures to My Students.* Grand Rapids: Zondervan, 1980.

Taylor, William. *Seven Years' Street Preaching in San Francisco.* London: Forgotten Books, 2015.

Tozer, A. W. *The Knowledge of the Holy.* New York: Harper & Row, 1961.

Van Til, Cornelius. *Christianity in Conflict.* Philadelphia: Westminster Theological Seminary, 1962–1964 (syllabus).

———. *An Introduction to Systematic Theology.* Nutley, N.J.: Presbyterian and Reformed, 1974.

———. *The Reformed Pastor and Modern Thought.* Nutley, N.J.: Presbyterian and Reformed, 1971.

Warnock, Adrian. "John Owen and Charles Spurgeon on John Bunyan." Patheos. October 24, 2007. http://www.patheos.com/blogs/adrianwarnock/2007/10/john-owen-and-charles-spurgeon-on-john/.

Wylie, J. A. *The History of Protestantism.* Vol. 1. London: Cassell & Company, 1880.